Is Henry Wallace a sincere idealist? Is he a man of great moral courage? Is he a fighter for the Common Man and the Common Man's Century?

This book pursues an objectively critical investigation into these and related subjects. It also answers other questions such as: Why did Henry Wallace purge the New Dealers from his Department of Agriculture in 1935? What were the "Zenda Letters" which threatened to put a Republican into the White House in 1940? Precisely what have been Wallace's relations with the Communists?

The answers given herein will not please Henry Wallace's admirers, but they will enlighten citizens who are called upon to support his candidacy for the White House.

This is the first full and frank examination of Mr. Wallace as a public figure. It is all the more impressive in that the criticism directed at the Iowa politician comes not from the Right but from the independent Left, which Mr. Wallace claims as his own.

HENRY WALLACE

THE MAN AND THE MYTH

by DWIGHT MACDONALD

"WHAT A MARVELOUS
OPPORTUNITY THERE IS
TODAY TO MINISTER
TO THE DISILLUSIONED
ONES!"
                HENRY WALLACE

New York. THE VANGUARD PRESS, INC.

This book is an elaboration of articles by the author published
in the March–April and May–June issues of *Politics*.

For Nancy

". . . Thou wouldst be great
Art not without ambition, but without
The illness should attend it: what thou wouldst highly,
That thou wouldst holily; wouldst not play false,
And yet wouldst wrongly win. Thou'dst have, great Glamis,
That which cries, 'Thus thou must do if thou have it,'
And that which rather thou dost fear to do
Than wishest should be undone."

Macbeth, Act I, scene 5

CONTENTS

1. The Wallace Myth

HENRY AGARD WALLACE is an ardent tennis-player. His form is said to be atrocious, but he makes up for awkwardness by energy, trying for everything and wearing his opponent down by sheer persistence. It is probably a canard that he once confessed to humanitarian compunctions about hitting the ball too hard. But the story is authentic that, after a hard-fought set, Wallace remarked to his defeated opponent: "I suppose it's not very Christian of me, but I *do* like to win." * The scruples, the clumsiness, the persistence, and the ambition are all characteristic of one of the most complex personalities in public life.

In other things beside tennis, Henry Wallace also likes to win. His old associate, Rexford Tugwell, once exclaimed, with a note of awe: "My God, that man's ambitious!" Since Tugwell himself was not precisely lacking in that quality, the tribute is all the more impressive. Henry Wallace has come far since the day in 1932 when Roosevelt plucked him from obscurity to make him his Secretary of Agriculture.

---

* These are his words as recalled by the opponent, one of Wallace's old associates. Throughout this book, references to printed sources are given either in the text or in the numbered "References" at the end. When material is not so identified, it is either because it seemed unnecessary (matters of common knowledge, newspaper reports in which the date is given, etc.) or else because, as here, it was obtained by interviews with persons having first-hand knowledge of the events.

The seven years in Agriculture, which made him a national figure as planner, prophet, and pamphleteer, were followed by the Vice-Presidency (1940–1944), a post in which his passionate rhetoric made him the Woodrow Wilson of World War II. The climax came at the Democratic 1944 convention, where Wallace—playing, as it turned out, for the highest stakes of all: the Presidency itself—was narrowly defeated by Truman for the vice-presidential nomination. There followed two rather blank years as Secretary of Commerce; then, in September, 1946, his forced resignation from the cabinet as the result of the celebrated Madison Square Garden speech; and now the editorship of *The New Republic,* a position that affords more scope for vanity than for ambition.

The end-result, to an ambitious man like Wallace, must be disappointing. At the present writing, Wallace commands about as much "grass-roots" following among the nation's farmers as Bruce Bliven. His wartime rhetoric, perhaps fortunately for him, is now forgotten. His overtures to the business community while Secretary of Commerce produced no discernible effects. The labor movement seems to have cooled toward him: three years ago, he was a keynote speaker at the C.I.O. convention, but in 1946 he was not invited, his place being filled by General Eisenhower. Even the liberals appear to be deserting him: the Progressive Citizens of America (P.C.A.), organized around Wallace in the fall of 1946, depends mostly on Hollywood for "names," while the bulk of more substantial liberal leaders—Eleanor Roosevelt, Ickes, Henderson, Bowles, Wyatt, to name a few—support the rival Americans for Democratic Action. The reason for the liberals' defection from the man they considered their national leader a short year ago is, of course, Wallace's pro-Russian stand in foreign policy and his involvement with the Communists in domestic politics.

It would seem, in short, as though Wallace had got himself into a political dead-end. As the antagonism between American and Russian imperialism increases—if, indeed, it can grow any sharper than it is now—the retreat from Moscow now going on in liberal-labor circles will become ever more precipitate. Yet Wallace is committed to a pro-Russian policy; he will squirm, he will evade and compromise, but it is hard to see how even his genius for obfuscation can extricate him.

There is perhaps no public figure so little understood by both his admirers and his enemies as Henry Wallace. This is because he is a split personality, an extraordinary combination of idealism and opportunism, moral fervor and *realpolitik,* bold challenge and timid evasion, and of any one of a dozen other antinomies which exist side by side within his personality. If one looks at Henry Wallace from the standpoint of what he says, one sees him as compounded of the first parts of the above contradictions: principled, sincere, morally courageous, etc. But if one looks at what he does (and also examines the obbligato, so to speak, of contradictory substatements that always accompany any major statement), then one sees him as compact of the second parts. Americans have been conditioned to think of words as acts—by advertising, by the demagogy of "Left" and "Right" alike, by the impossibility of getting behind a politician's words, in this large-scale society, without more trouble than most people can or will take. Hence

it has been Wallace's words to which both friends and
enemies have paid most attention, with confusing results.

A myth has grown up around Wallace, a myth which his
political opponents have accepted as uncritically as his followers have. On the occasion of his nomination for Vice-
President, for example, even the conservative *New York
Times* editorialized: "Whatever distrust of or opposition
to his policies there may be, it is always accompanied by
respect and esteem for the man. In more than ten years
of public service, he has raised no crop of enemies. His
integrity, sincerity, disinterestedness and goodwill are manifest to all."

What is the Wallace Myth? As we follow his career, we
shall examine it in detail. Here let us attempt a summary
confrontation of image and reality.

FICTION #1: *That Wallace is a man of notable integrity.*

FACT: Even on the modest scale required of politicians, he
rates low. For example:

(a) In addressing the Congress of American-Soviet
Friendship on November 8, 1942, Wallace quoted De
Tocqueville as follows: "There are at the present time two
great nations of the world which seem to tend toward the
same end, although they start from different points. I allude
to the Russians and the Americans. [The American struggles against nature, the Russian against his fellow-men.
. . . To gain his end, the American relies on personal interest, permitting the strength and intelligence of individuals to have free play without control from above. But
the Russian concentrates in one man the whole power of
society. The one has for its principal means of action
Liberty; the other, Servitude.] Their starting-point is dif-

ferent and their course is not the same, yet each of them seems to be marked by the will of heaven to sway the destinies of half the globe." The sentences in brackets were omitted by Wallace.

(b) The split in the liberal ranks in the fall of 1946 was a source of great anxiety to Wallace, since almost all the "big names" went into the Americans for Democratic Action (A.D.A.)—which bars Communists from membership—leaving him isolated as leader of the P.C.A. On January 27, 1947, he wrote in *The New Republic:* "The point I want to make is that the liberals today in the so-called warring groups are about 90 per cent in agreement. Some people who have read about 'Mrs. Roosevelt's A.D.A. and Henry Wallace's P.C.A.' have written in, asking, 'How does it happen that Henry Wallace and Mrs. Roosevelt are in warring camps?' The answer is: 'We are not.' I am not a member of the P.C.A. and Mrs. Roosevelt, to the best of my knowledge, is not a member or an officer of the A.D.A. I spoke to one organization urging unity in the progressive ranks. Mrs. Roosevelt spoke to the other." It is technically true that Wallace is not a member of the P.C.A., though a larger concept of truth would embrace the facts that he made the keynote speech at P.C.A.'s founding convention, that P.C.A. is built around only one man, Henry Wallace, and that he speaks for P.C.A. in full-page newspaper ads. But Mrs. Roosevelt *was* a member of A.D.A., as Wallace could have found out by a call to her or to A.D.A., or a perusal of the newspapers. His whole picture of the A.D.A.-P.C.A. split, based on a false statement, was thus misleading. The next day Mrs. Roosevelt publicly reaffirmed her membership in A.D.A. No correction was made by Wallace nor by *The New Republic*.

(c) On July 23, 1946, while he was still Secretary of Commerce, Wallace wrote a letter to President Truman criticizing American policy toward Russia, especially as to the atomic bomb. His main points, which simply repeated the Russian position on the bomb, were that the American proposals for atomic disarmament were unilateral, in that other nations would have to disarm without the United States being in any way committed to do so, that the veto issue was "irrelevant," and that the Russian counter-proposal "in some respects goes even farther than our plan and is in agreement with the basic principles of our plan." The letter was made public by Truman on September 17. Bernard Baruch, author of the American plan, met with Wallace and his aides on September 27 and apparently convinced him that his criticism flowed from ignorance of the American proposals. The conference ended with Wallace's aides drawing up a letter, to be signed by him, admitting that "at the time I wrote my letter to the President, I was not fully posted on some aspects of the position of the United States Representative." When it came to signing the letter, however, Wallace simply vanished for three days (a common habit in crises); finally, he telephoned Baruch that he would agree to sign only an entirely different letter in which, far from conceding ignorance and error, he gave the impression that he had been right, that Baruch had also been right, and that everybody agreed with everybody. Baruch, being a reactionary, resented this doubletalk, broke off negotiations, and made the whole thing public, with texts. Wallace, being a progressive, republished his original letter to Truman, with none of the misstatements corrected, in a pamphlet entitled "The Fight for Peace."

(d) Few politicians make such uninhibited use of the "smear" technique. In both the 1940 and the 1944 campaigns he was the only top-ranking Democrat who dared to reduce the issues to the level: "A vote for Willkie (or Dewey) is a vote for Hitler." Nor does he retract his smears when they are shown to be without foundation. Thus, on February 23, 1943, he charged that a prominent Republican leader had advised Wilson, in October, 1917, to send only food and arms abroad, no soldiers. "His advice would have allowed Germany to win the war in 1917. This man, in perfectly good faith, is giving similar advice today. He would cut down the size of our army regardless of military necessities." Although the Republican was carefully not named, it was clear that Hoover was meant. On March 2, Hoover replied that (1) he had advised a slowing-down of inductions because, as he had stated at the time, more men were being enrolled than could be trained at once and because manpower was badly needed in war industries; and (2) his advice to Wilson had been in the form of a memo to Colonel House, which he had in his files, and that its date had been not October but February, 1917—i.e., it had been written before the United States entered the war. He challenged Wallace either to prove his assertions or to retract them. Wallace did neither.

(e) On November 1, 1945, when the General Motors strike was imminent, Wallace, as Secretary of Commerce, made public a confidential report by the Department's economists which demonstrated that industrial wages could be raised by 10 per cent without any price advance. The report greatly strengthened the union's position and was a crucial factor in the strike settlement. Four months later, when events had somewhat undermined the economic basis of the report, Wallace said that of course it was not meant to be taken as an official document; apparently, some of his economists had just been thinking out loud. But it had not occurred to him to indicate the report's unofficial character at the time when it made a difference.

FICTION #2: *That Wallace has great moral courage.*

FACT: Throughout his career, Wallace has backed down when the opposition was strong, has altered his sentiments to placate his audience, has run away from a fight on principles whenever he could. For example:

(a) As Secretary of Agriculture in 1935, he "purged" the New Dealers when pressure was put on him by big business and the spokesmen for the well-to-do farmers.

(b) During the delivery of his Madison Square Garden speech in the fall of 1946, the fellow-travelers who packed the hall booed at one or two mildly critical remarks about Russian policy. Wallace was visibly upset; for the rest of the speech, he simply omitted, from the typed copy before him, all uncomplimentary references to Russia. Asked why later, he replied: "Because I felt I had been booed enough. I didn't see any particular point in making a riot there."

(c) Businessmen as well as Communists intimidate Wallace. When he addressed the American Business Congress in 1943, he omitted the following sentence, which appeared in the transcript released to the press: "The present high concentration of investment banking in New York is itself incompatible with free enterprise, for only large national corporations have access on reasonable terms to that market." It is perhaps superfluous to note that the Congress was held in New York.[1] *

(d) In Wallace's book *Statesmanship and Religion* (1934), based on lectures, there occurs on page forty-five a humorous reference to the Anti-Popery of his forefathers. A footnote informs us that, when the lectures were syndicated for newspaper publication, Wallace had asked that this passage be dropped, but by mistake it was not. "It is obvious," adds the note, "that the author wishes to emphasize those things which unite humanity rather than those which separate." It might also have added that the lectures were delivered to Protestant groups, while the syndicated articles would have been read by Catholics as well. The author, in general, has always wished to emphasize those things which unite humanity—to him.

(e) In 1935, Wallace was engaged in a sharp controversy with the New England textile manufacturers, who objected to the A.A.A. processing tax on cotton. On April 17, he made a speech in Maine in which he asked, "Where is the rugged individualism I've heard so much about?" and commented on "whining that doesn't do any credit to New England ingenuity" and "the flabbiness of the third and fourth generations." There was a great uproar throughout New England. It was an awkward moment, with a presidential election due next year, so, on April 24, Wallace wrote the president of the New England Council repudiating his statements and charging the press with misquotation. If Bryan was the Great Commoner, Wallace is the Great Misquotee. Reporters never seem to get his remarks straight, especially when they turn out to have been ill-advised.

* Numerals indicate references given at the end of the book.

FICTION #3: *That he is a dreamer, a visionary whose spirit moves in realms far above petty political considerations.*

FACT: It is true that Wallace is a clumsy political operator, but this is not because he is too pure for this world but because of a constitutional fuzziness of judgment for which he earnestly tries to compensate by allying himself to extremely "realistic" groups and individuals. Thus, while he was Secretary of Agriculture, he worked closely with the powerful (and anti-New Deal) Farm Bureau lobby. As Vice-President and Secretary of Commerce, he selected as his political mentor a conventional ward-politician type, Harold Young (of whom more later). Of late, he has become more and more deeply involved with the Stalinists, as ruthless and realistic a crew as ever rigged an election or weaseled a resolution. That he is not conspicuously successful as a *realpolitiker* is due to lack of talent, not effort.

FICTION #4: *That Wallace is rigid, even somewhat doctrinaire, in his ideology.*

FACT: He is a man not of principle but of principles—all of them all together all at once. He preaches the economics of abundance and plows under every third row. He prepares for the coming Century of the Common Man by helping plan the atomic bomb. His views on materialistic progress would be equally pleasing to Tolstoy and Herbert Spencer, depending on which paragraph each happened to read. He favors State control and planning of economy, but is careful also to praise Free Enterprise. His book *Sixty Million Jobs* (1945) was generally taken as a manifesto for New Deal planning and spending, but closer inspection

shows that it calls for a balanced budget, business tax re-
ductions, no Planned Economy, and little more State
spending than most business groups were then recommend-
ing. As for Free Enterprise, it turns out to be synonymous
with full employment: "The full-employment problem—
which, after all, is the preservation of our democratic free
enterprise system." But if he is not a fanatical Planner,
neither is he a fanatical Free Enterpriser. He believes, in
fact, in Eric Johnston's now-forgotten "people's capitalism,"
that is, a system of economic privilege in which *everyone* is
a member of the elite. As for the class struggle, he wants
everybody to win it. "We must find, and find it soon," he
declared in June, 1947, "some effective means of protecting
the general welfare—and doing this even as we strengthen,
instead of weaken, the rights and interests of both manage-
ment and labor." [2] No, Henry Wallace is not doctrinaire.

FICTION #5: *That Wallace has fought the good fight
against privilege and injustice.*

FACT: One of the most striking things about Wallace's
career is how much talking he has done about fighting for
the Common Man, and how little acting. He has occupied
posts of great power, but has been chary of putting his words
into action. As Secretary of Agriculture, he let Tugwell,
Frank, and others do the fighting for the "under-privileged." As a top figure in the war economy, he did engage
in a strenuous conflict with conservatives like Hull and
Jesse Jones, but the issue was the efficient conduct of the
war; this seems to have little to do with the interests of the
Common Man (though efficiency now seems to be becoming, as in Russia, a criterion of liberalism). As Secretary
of Commerce, he made no significant reforms and chose

conservative businessmen for his top aides. All through his career, Wallace has avoided a fight wherever he could (and sometimes where he couldn't). For example:

(a) During the filibuster of Southern Senators against the Poll Tax Bill in 1942, Wallace, as Vice-President, presided over the Senate. Certain liberal Senators, including the late George W. Norris, urged Wallace to dramatize the issue by not leaving the chair, sleeping there if necessary. This might have had some practical value as well: parliamentary opportunities might have occurred to end the filibuster. Wallace, however, refused to co-operate, turning the chair over to any handy Senator whenever he got tired.

(b) One of Wallace's habitual strategies when confronted with a conflict is simply to be somewhere else. This was his tactic in the 1935 "purge" in the Department of Agriculture and in the controversy with Baruch about the atomic bomb. During the nation-wide effort to get a reprieve for Odell Waller, the Negro sharecropper who killed his white landlord in a fight and who was executed for what would normally have been a manslaughter case, a delegation of Negro and White liberals called on Wallace to ask him to intervene with Roosevelt. They were shown into the office of Wallace's lieutenant, Harold Young, who received them with his feet on the desk and a cigar in his mouth. Without removing either, he informed them, in a Southern drawl, that the Common Man's Friend was not in, and that, anyway, nothing could be done about their request. As they were filing out, they caught sight of Wallace leaving his office. Embarrassed, the tribune of the people put on speed. But the delegation included Mrs. Mary McLeod Bethune, a woman of considerable determination. Although she walks with difficulty, using a cane, she hobbled after him, calling out loudly, "Oh, Mr. Wallace, I want to talk to you!" At which Wallace walked even faster, saying over his shoulder, "There's nothing I can do in the matter, Mrs. Bethune." Stories differ as to whether the pursuit was successful or not, but in any case the delegation got no help or sympathy from Wallace. He was, officially and spiritually, Elsewhere.

(c) The late President Roosevelt, who, whatever his shortcomings, was a shrewd judge of men, said to James A. Farley in 1938: "Henry Wallace would like to run for President. However, I'd rather have a fellow like Ickes, who, at least, is a fighter. Ickes will go through with whatever he has in mind. But you never know what Henry will do. He's in favor of one thing today and something entirely different tomorrow."

At this point, two questions arise: How has the Wallace myth survived so long? What qualities of his have made him so prominent a leader of the liberal-labor movement? The answers are to be found in the realm of language. Wallace has made a career by supplying to the liberals a commodity they crave: rhetoric which accomplishes in fantasy what cannot be accomplished in reality. His relation to them is comparable to that of Hitler to the German middle classes: a demagogue whose rhetoric to an outside observer appears to be stylistically atrocious and intellectually puerile, but which strikes through to certain deep, confused mass emotions. Fortunately, the liberals are not so large or significant a class as the middle classes, and Wallace apparently lacks *charisma* (or political sex-appeal) for a wider

American audience. As Roosevelt once remarked: "Henry just hasn't got It."

HIS IMPERSONAL IDIOM: WALLESE

Wallaceland is the mental habitat of Henry Wallace plus a few hundred thousand regular readers of *The New Republic, The Nation,* and *PM.* It is a region of perpetual fogs, caused by the warm winds of the liberal Gulf Stream coming in contact with the Soviet glacier. Its natives speak "Wallese," a debased provincial dialect.

Wallese is as rigidly formalized as Mandarin Chinese. The Good people are described by ritualistic adjectives: "forward-looking," "freedom-loving," "clear-thinking," and, of course, "democratic" and "progressive." The Bad people are always "reactionaries" or "Red-baiters"; there are surprisingly few of them, considering the power they wield, and they are perversely wicked, since their *real* interests would best be served by the Progressive and Realistic policies favored by the Good people. Wallese is always employed to Unite rather than to Divide (hence the fog), and to Further Positive, Constructive Aims rather than Merely to Engage in Irresponsible and Destructive Criticism. As George F. Babbitt of Zenith City, who had his own brand of Wallese in the twenties, used to say: It's Easy Enough to Criticize! There are other conventions in Wallese. Issues are always Clarified, Events invariably Exert Pressure, Problems are Faced (good) or Not Faced (bad), and the World is either On the March (good) or At the Crossroads (neutral) or Facing a Crisis (bad). No article may be composed in Wallese unless it includes at least one of the following terms: "grass roots," "integration," "horizon," "general welfare." The frequent use of the "should and will" or "can and must" construction is also obligatory, as in the (imaginary) sentence: "The American people can and must free the forward march of technology from the dead hand of monopoly." The adjective "new" is much used, as: "new horizons," "new frontiers," and "the new democracy" (which means the old democracy minus all democratic elements). Like "adventure," another important word in Wallese, it suggests something Different (and God knows we're sick of what we've got now), Positive, Exciting—something to which the old critical categories, which have proved so lethal in the hands of Irresponsible and Destructive critics, cannot be applied. Thus many of us are by now somewhat leery of both democracy and *The New Republic,* but how about the *new* democracy and the new *New Republic?* Perhaps the greatest sentence ever composed in Wallese is the following, from the hand of the master himself: "New frontiers beckon with meaningful adventure."

Wallese is not, of course, Henry Wallace's personal idiom. There is nothing personal about his writing—indeed, alienation from his own individual interests, values, and enjoyment is the most striking thing about Wallace's whole "style" as a political figure. Unlike Churchill or Roosevelt, for example, who clearly got a big kick out of exercising power and hurling around the thunderbolts of political rhetoric, Wallace is lumpish, depressed, weighed down by a sense of duty (or of guilt?). His political personality curiously resembles Herbert Hoover's. "The words that spring from his mind," writes an admirer, "sometimes stumbling, sometimes leaping, are those of a man troubled, deeply troubled by the far-reaching sickness of these times. He takes little pride in his writing. . . . 'Strangely enough, I don't like to write,' he says." [3] As literary criticism, nothing could be wider of the mark: Wallace's words don't spring, they don't leap, and they don't even stumble; they just ooze. But it is true that his writing is that of a sick and troubled man, a man not at peace with himself, alienated from his own individuality, a man who doesn't enjoy writing because he senses obscurely that it has nothing to do with his own pleasure and convictions.

Wallese is a collective product, a style that has developed in liberal journalism more or less instinctively as a drapery for the harsh political realities of our time. The justification for calling it "Wallese" is that Henry Wallace has parlayed it into a career.

This is not to say that Wallace is an accomplished rhetorician, as, for example, Churchill is. On the contrary, he is a ghastly stylist by the most modest journalistic standards: dull, vague, repetitious, humorless, with a fatal affinity for the cliché. His rule is never to use one word where ten will do the job. Mrs. Roosevelt has said that Wallace reads better than he sounds in person; I have not heard him speak publicly, but I cannot believe this is an accurate statement. His tone is that of the principal of a progressive school addressing a parent-teacher meeting: "The job of reconciling Jeffersonian democracy to the impact of machine civilization is one which is going to take the most imaginative resources of all of us." [4] He begins a series of lectures, which were published in 1938 under the Wallesian title, *Paths to Plenty*: "In these lectures, I propose to consider the way in which the best elements in capitalism, democracy and religion can cooperate to lay a foundation for the long-term general welfare."

As the above sentence shows, the defects of his style are not only esthetic. Wallace never analyzes a problem: he barges around inside it, throwing out vague exhortations. The sentence quoted could have meaning only if Wallace defined the abstractions which comprise its entire content. But he continues: "Throughout this book, I have used the phrase, 'general welfare,' liberally. . . . Nowhere have I defined 'general welfare' . . . because I believe that in a democracy every individual ought to define the general welfare in his own way." This is perhaps the most revealing statement Wallace ever wrote. Aside from the absurdity of refusing to define one's terms on the grounds that this would violate the democratic right of each citizen to read his own definition into them—a right Hitler always respected—it shows us why Wallace represses his own self in politics. The self-alienation is evident: if every individual has a right "to define the general welfare in his own way," then Wallace has the right. But he gives it up, as he gives up other personal rights and pleasures (such as the right to speak the truth and the pleasure of sticking to one's principles) because he wants to make himself an instrument through which "the common man" (i.e., everybody) expresses himself. If he defined terms, some people would be antagonistic; but Wallace wants to be loved, and followed, by *everybody,* just as he wants to believe every doctrine all at once. This tendency reaches its height in the matter of "the general welfare," for here is the key Wallese concept: a noun no one could possibly object to (for who but a fascist or Red-baiter could be perversely *against* welfare?)

wedded to an adjective that is . . . general. The whole suggests a bold stand for the common man against his enemies, thus combining the maximum of safety with the maximum of emotive force. It is understandable that Henry Wallace would not want to endanger such a concept by defining it.

The political ideas expressed in Wallese are as amorphous as the idiom itself. In the grand tradition of American politics, Henry works both sides of the street. Although the Wallace Myth, accepted by critics and admirers alike, sees him as a Planner at home and an Internationalist abroad, an examination of his speeches and writings shows that he has been careful to offset every tribute to Planning with a salute to Free Enterprise, and to balance his pleas for a daily quart of milk for every inhabitant of the globe with equally impassioned defenses of American imperialism.

Wallace's political ideology may be treated under three heads: 1. Henry Wallace, Free Enterpriser; 2. Henry Wallace, Imperialist; 3. Henry Wallace, State Capitalist. The connection between the first two and the last is closer than might appear: certain collective disciplines, working through a strong central State, are to be superimposed on the present American System, to which Wallace is as loyal as Senator Taft. The non-Wallesian term for this kind of society is State Capitalism.

1. Henry Wallace, Free Enterpriser

"The spirit of competition will and must continue to be one of our main driving forces," Wallace stated recently. "Individual initiative and enterprise and government responsibility for the general welfare will continue to pull in double harness for a better life for our people. Horatio Alger is not dead and never will be.* My vision is of an America where all can become members of the middle class, where all can share in the benefits which that class has enjoyed in the past." [6] It is not clear whether Wallace thinks that "individual enterprise" and "government responsibility for the general welfare" are or are not at present "pulling in double harness" for everybody's benefit: the Wallesian "will and must" construction successfully obscures this crucial point. The implication is that while the system is good, it can (and must) be even better. Which reminds one of Dunsany's house agent who tells prospective tenants: "If it weren't for the plumbing this would be the best house in London." When the customer asks what's wrong with the plumbing, the reply is: "The plumbing is good, too, but not as good as the house."

In a later article, printed in *The Saturday Evening Post* under the unimprovable title "We Must Save Free Enterprise," Wallace draws a metaphysical distinction between the "real" or "inner" nature of capitalism and the "perversions" of that nature which capitalists have committed.[7] He shows that the actual history of American capitalism, evolving as it has toward big-business monopoly, is simply an illusion; and that the little businessmen who have been eliminated from most of the economy are the "true" representatives of the capitalist spirit. The corner grocer put out of business by the chain stores and the little steel fabricator

---

* A recent survey of twenty thousand New York City children between the ages of eight and fourteen showed that 92 per cent had never heard of Horatio Alger and that fewer than 1 per cent had read any of his books. [5]

driven to the wall by United States Steel may thus console themselves that their bankruptcies are unreal and that they, not their successful rivals, represent the capitalist "essence." Or, in Wallese: "Capitalism throughout the world and even in our own country has often been the object of derision. Not its inherent faults but its misuses have been the underlying reason for this attitude. Considered in its essentials, however, capitalism can be the most efficient system of organizing products and distribution on principles of freedom and equal opportunity yet devised by man." The impact of this Hegelian distinction between the "essential" and the "apparent" is somewhat diminished when Wallace goes on to enumerate the formidable list of reforms which must be brought about to realize the true, inner nature of capitalism. These include Full Employment, Full Production, No More Monopolies, the Revival of Small Business, the Development of New Frontiers, and an Economy of Abundance. The author's approval of these worthy goals is considerably more explicit than his notion of how to reach them.

The article also pays tribute to the notion of a "people's capitalism," which had just been advanced by Eric Johnston, then head of the United States Chamber of Commerce and now Will Hays's successor in Hollywood. As outlined in the *Readers Digest* under the (also unimprovable) title "Three Kinds of Capitalism—Which Offers a Poor Boy the Best Chance?," this is a class system in which everyone belongs to the ruling class—"an ultimate capitalism for everybody" is Mr. Johnston's formulation.[8] "I come from it. I want to see it survive for every poor boy and girl in America after me." The general idea is that there are now three kinds of capitalism, and that the only Good kind, providentially enough, is to be found right here in the United States of America. The listing is: (1) State Capitalism (Russia), (2) Monopoly Capitalism (England), (3) People's Capitalism (United States). Despite certain theoretical difficulties—as, if everybody becomes a capitalist, who will operate the plants which make the dividends on which everybody lives?—it was a generous and, to an American, inspiring concept, and well worthy to stand along Wallace's own formulations of "the people's war" and "the people's century."

2. Henry Wallace, Imperialist

To Free Enterprise at home, Wallace adds Imperialism abroad—what might be called "popular imperialism" or, perhaps, "the imperialism of the common man." A British admirer recently defined Wallace's "chief contribution" while Secretary of Commerce as: "the perception that backward societies must be brought toward industrialization. . . . Wallace proposed that it should become the chief function and glory of American industry to equip such countries with machinery. . . . In other words, he is an internationalist who can see beyond his own frontiers. That is what the little minds mean who called him 'a starry-eyed idealist.' " [9] By this yardstick, Eugene Grace of Bethlehem Steel and Thomas W. Lamont of J. P. Morgan, both of whom have long considered it their chief function and glory to equip backward countries with machinery, at a price, are internationalists and in imminent danger of denunciation as starry-eyed idealists.

Although Wallace's slogan, "The People's Century," was

evolved as a counter to Henry Luce's "The American Century," it is difficult to find significant differences between the two. Luce wrote:

"The vision of America as the dynamic leader of world trade has within it the possibilities of such enormous human progress as to stagger the imagination. Let us not be staggered by it. Let us rise to its possibilities. . . . We think of Asia as being worth only a few hundred millions a year to us. Actually, in the decades to come, Asia will be worth to us exactly zero—or else, four, five, ten billions a year. And the latter are the terms in which we must think, or else confess a pitiable impotence." [10]

Luce's article was immediately damned by the liberals, beginning with Henry Wallace, as Reactionary, Imperialistic, Nationalistic, etc. What they were really objecting to, however, was not what Luce said but the way he said it. Being a reactionary, Luce put things bluntly, without the doubletalk to which liberals are accustomed. Not long after Luce's article appeared, Milo Perkins, Wallace's chief lieutenant and closest associate during the war years, gave his own vision of the American Century. The language is more tactful, but the theme is identical:

"Mr. Perkins advances many arguments in favor of his thesis. He points out the great new market that would be opened by the industrialization of Asia, of India, of Africa. He notes that by increasing the income of the people of Asia by one penny a day there would be created a new four-billion-dollars-a-year market. He adds that it staggers comprehension to picture the vast markets that would be established if it were possible to provide the peoples of the world with merely the minimum of food and shelter." [11]

It might be noted that both Luce and Perkins-Wallace would benefit by reading such readily available works as Marx's *Capital* and the studies of imperialism made by Lenin and by Hobson. They write as though up to now no one had suspected the existence of these vast potential markets in Asia and other backward lands. The contrary is, however, the fact: for generations capitalists have been struggling to develop these colonial markets, just as American entrepreneurs have long been aware of the almost unlimited internal market which exists, also potentially, within the borders of even a relatively prosperous country like the United States. The difficulty is that capitalism, which all three are agreed is to be retained, just doesn't seem to have evolved the magic formula to permit the worker-producers to be paid enough to buy back the products of their labor. So the Asiatic market is still potential and shows few signs of advancing beyond that hypothetical stage.*

Wallace was equally uninformed when he declared, in 1942, that after the war "older nations will have the privilege to help younger nations get started on the path to industrialization." Older nations have always had that privilege, and have exercised it freely, at profits of 50 per cent up. "There must be no imperialism," says Wallace, but he does not specify what motive, under Free Enterprise, will replace the profit spur in spreading industrialization.

* Apropos of the Luce-Perkins dream of Asia, it is interesting to note that the final effort of the Chamberlain government to turn Hitler aside from war was the Hudson-Wohltat conference in August, 1939, in which Britain invited Germany to a joint exploitation, financed by Britain, of the Chinese market. Hitler and his advisers preferred the risks of war to the risks of such an enterprise.

Of late, Wallace has added two original concepts: Technocratic Imperialism and Ruthful Imperialism.

The former he developed in a radio speech during his visit to England. Advocating the application of "the technique of the Tennessee Valley Authority to the Valley of the Jordan" and the use of "the resources of modern science to transform the sandy desert that lies between the Tigris and the Euphrates once again into the Garden of Eden," he observes: "If we brought water and power to serve the people of these arid wastes, no one would grudge us the oil that we need. We would not be imperialists, but technicians, enabling these people to develop more fruitfully and healthfully their own way of life, not in terms of graft for the few, but with the aim of prosperity for all who are willing to work, to study and learn. And thus we should do our part to develop peaceful citizens rather than revolutionaries with reason to be suspicious of our intentions. The whole world needs a New Deal and there will be no peace till it has one." [12]

The effect of this Wallesian vision was slightly impaired when, speaking a few weeks later in Paris, Wallace advanced the idea of Ruthful Imperialism. "He added that former President Roosevelt had sought and the Navy had demanded oil of Saudi Arabia, although the U.S.A. had half the world's oil already. 'Nobody will stop us, and yet this is imperialism and to this extent the United States is proud of it. It is not ruthless imperialism but good old-fashioned American imperialism.' " [13] The criterion here is not whether T.V.A.'s and Gardens of Eden spring up in the wake of Standard Oil, but simply whether it is the United States or some other country which is making eyes

at colonial resources. If the latter, the imperialism is ruthless; if the former, it is what Wallace genially calls the
"good old-fashioned American" variety. On Arabian oil, indeed, Wallace is entirely sound. His affectionate tolerance
for Stalin's regime stops short at Saudi Arabia. He was recently quoted as saying that if Russia attempted to expand
to central Turkey "and thus threaten Saudi Arabian oil,"
Britain and the United States "should fight" (later amended
to "would fight").[14] He hoped, he added, that his statement
"would get back to Russia."

Mr. Wallace, meet Mr. Luce.

3. Henry Wallace, State Capitalist.

Wallace's endorsement of capitalism is sometimes taken
to be in conflict with his enthusiasm for State planning and
control. The contradiction, however, is only superficial.
Since he does not favor any radical change in society—
whether socialist, communist, or anarchist—Wallace's liberalism simply means that he looks to the State instead of
to Business as the motor of capitalism. "Social discipline"
in the interests of "the general welfare" is the essence of his
political philosophy.

There are many indications of this attitude. As when, in
the spring of 1946, he suggested that all Democratic Congressmen who did not follow the party line in their votes
in Congress should be expelled from the party. Or when,
after the 1946 coal strike, he recommended public ownership of industries where "the welfare of the whole country
is damaged to an unendurable degree by repeated strikes,"
adding: "In such a case, the workers in that industry
would, like other federal employees, give up the right to

. . . strike." Or when, during the 1944 campaign, he said: "There is no peacetime job for profit or self which ever again will be paramount over the needs of all. Government service must be the supreme duty when the need is determined. There can be no slackers as we fight for the common man in his pursuit of the richer life."

The economic term for this is State Capitalism. The political term is Totalitarian Liberalism. This latter may seem a hopelessly contradictory term. A "liberal" used to be one who favored the spread of liberty: freedom of thought, more humane economic arrangements, the "popular" cause in general against kings or bankers or governments. Today it has become one who favors the extension of governmental authority for reasons of efficiency, especially in wartime. The modern liberal generally calls himself a "progressive," a semantically interesting shift from a term which implies *values* to a term which implies *process*.

The old liberals of the last century were dangerous men, devoted to high ideals and willing to challenge established institutions. Tom Paine and Mazzini are examples. Later on, the passion and the effectiveness shifted over to the Marxists and anarchists; the liberals of the early twentieth century became increasingly ineffectual, mildly benevolent figures, trying to straddle the basic issues. Norman Thomas and Oswald Garrison Villard are examples. Of late years, a third type has become dominant: the liberal *realpolitiker,* the "social engineer" who Gets Things Done and thinks in terms of the efficient conduct of modern mass-society. Fiorello LaGuardia and Henry Wallace are examples.

The first type was principled and effective, the second

principled and ineffective, the third is unprincipled and effective.

In the great modern debate on the individual vs. the State, Henry Wallace is far out on the side of the State even for a Type 3, or Totalitarian, liberal. His acceptance of Soviet Russia as a "progressive" society is only one instance.

His writings are rich in expressions of Type 3 liberalism. As: "The general welfare has ultimate significance only insofar as it expresses itself in the individual welfare, and the individual gains his fullest and richest experiences when he . . . merges into the activity of the whole organism. . . . In the era of general welfare which we are now entering, there will be an ever-increasing knowledge and conscience with regard to group rights and group duties." [15] In short, the individual lives most richly when he "merges into the activity of the whole organism."

The messianic strain in Wallace fits in smoothly with his totalitarian liberalism. This came out with special clarity during the war. As the editors of *The Christian Century* observed:

"In many ways, Mr. Wallace is fitted to become the high priest of a new religion of nationalism. . . . Throughout the address [Wallace's speech before the Foreign Policy Association on April 8, 1941] the war was presented as a struggle between angels who have no need for penitence and devils beyond redemption, between noonday white and midnight black. . . .

"The unexpressed major premise was that the maintenance of order is the supreme good and that the procedures of international war can overcome evil, create right and justice and build democracy at home. Indeed, the only elements in the 'Bill of Duties' which Mr. Wallace set up for youth to parallel the Bill of Rights were that youth 'fight' and that he enlist to 'keep order. Modern civilization, in order to continue, must have order.' The climax of youth's effort would be 'an international order sufficiently strong to prevent the rise of aggressor nations.' . . .

"The religious trend evident in the mind of the Vice-President . . . by making a particular application of the tenets of the Thomist view of the State to the present situation, seems to us to be headed straight toward blessing unlimited and totalitarian war by religion. . . . Mr. Wallace seems primarily concerned with the survival of the State. . . . The final end of this point of view, as Mr. Wallace suggests in his reference to the '*pax democratica* which will bless us and the whole world for a century to come,' is that its messianism becomes imperialism." [16]

2. The Secretary of Agriculture
(1933–1940)

T HE PERSONAL EVOLUTION of Henry Wallace
was nicely rounded out when *The New York Times*
for February 26, 1947, announced that he was changing
his legal residence from Iowa to New York. Evolution is perhaps not the best word. Devolution might be better, considering that a competent corn breeder has become an inept
editorialist and an honest crop statistician a fisher in the
muddy waters of Stalinism.

THE IOWAN BACKGROUND

The place to begin to understand Henry Wallace is with
his grandfather, of the same name. "Uncle Henry," as he
was known to everyone, was born on the Western frontier of Pennsylvania in 1836, the son of a Scotch-Irish
farmer who had emigrated from Ireland a few years earlier.
Becoming a Presbyterian minister, he served as chaplain in
the Civil War. Tuberculosis, a family weakness, forced
him to give up the ministry and move west to the healthier
climate of Iowa, where he became a farmer. He made a
success of it, came to own several farms, and to edit and
partly own a farm paper. In 1895, at the age of sixty, he
really began his career: he quarreled with the other owners

39

of the paper, who thought he was attacking the trusts too vigorously, and left to found his own paper, *Wallace's Farmer*. Published in Des Moines, Iowa, this soon became one of the most widely read farm papers in the country; it combined religion and agronomy, being respected for the soundness of its views on infant damnation and on hog cholera. Uncle Henry wrote a regular Sunday Lesson every week which was one of the most popular features of the paper; he piled up enough in advance for them to keep appearing for years after he died in 1918. But he was more than a rural pietist. Tall, bearded, with a fine presence, he had wit, character, and backbone; he was a natural leader. Nationally prominent as a farm spokesman, he is said to have twice refused the Secretaryship of Agriculture. Like his grandson, he was a prolific writer. Three titles suggest his range: *Clover Culture; Trusts and How to Deal with Them; The Doctrines of the Plymouth Brethren*. At least one of his books is still extremely good reading: his simple, concrete description of how people ate, washed, worked, slept, and amused themselves in the frontier Pennsylvania of his boyhood.[17] Sociologists and children should both find it fascinating. All in all, Uncle Henry was the kind of simple, strong, shrewd personality which the republic once produced but which rarely appears now; the contrast is strong with his grandson, who has many of his superficial traits and little of his inner strength.

Wallace's father, Henry Cantwell Wallace, inherited Uncle Henry's strong character but seems to have lacked his spark of personality. Born in 1866, he ran the family farms for a while, later becoming professor of dairying at Iowa State Agricultural College at Ames, Iowa, and finally

succeeding his father as editor of *Wallace's Farmer*. Like
his father, he was a leader of the Midwest farmers against
the railroads and the monopolies: for seventeen years he
was secretary of the Corn Belt Meat Producers Association,
which fought against the Chicago meat packers; and he
was also prominent in the struggle to get lower railroad
rates on farm products. There was nothing at all radical
about these activities: the Wallaces, as one of the more prosperous families in Des Moines, were solid Republicans and
had as little use for Bryan and the Populists as for the pack-
ing trust. *Wallace's Farmer* supported McKinley in the crucial election of 1896 and profited much from the campaign
advertising put out by Mark Hanna's headquarters. Like
his father, Henry II was a Presbyterian, being especially
active in Y.M.C.A. work. He served as Secretary of Agriculture under Harding and Coolidge, but the office which
made his son a national figure was for the father an unhappy experience. The Republicans were the party of big
business, and Hoover, the most influential cabinet member,
blocked Wallace's attempts to get "farm relief" through
such financially unorthodox methods as McNary-Haughenism. It was too early for the farmer to get consideration in
Washington. When he died in office in 1924, Henry II was
a frustrated and defeated man.

Henry Agard Wallace was born in 1888, while his father
was teaching at Ames. He followed in the family tradition,
winning a "champion plowboy" medal at the age of twelve.
The well-known Negro botanist, George Washington
Carver, who was a student and friend of Professor Wallace,
used to take the young Henry on long walks in the coun-

try, arousing his interest in plant breeding. Wallace was
graduated from Ames in 1910, took a trip to Europe in
1912, and married an Iowa girl, Ilo Browne, in 1914. His
biographer describes an odd episode after the wedding:
"As they left the church to drive to the reception, he [Wal-
lace] entered the car ahead of his bride, closed the door
before he thought, and left her standing there for several
seconds, until the gibes of onlookers reminded him that he
was no longer a single man." [18] Whatever significance this
may have, if any, the marriage seems to be a happy one.

Soon after he got out of college, the young Wallace began to experiment with corn breeding. He observed that at
state fairs the most regularly formed ears of corn won the
prizes; he questioned this criterion on the reasonable
grounds that a hog has no sense of beauty. His own experiments, which included a good deal of inbreeding, produced
ears which were not lovely to look at but which were superior in more important factors such as hardiness and
abundant yield. Out of these experiments came the Hi-
Bred Corn Company, of Des Moines, which built up a
prosperous business selling seed corn to farmers. This company, in which Wallace still owns a minority interest, is
said to do an annual business of several million dollars.
Wallace's income from Hi-Bred has been estimated at fifty
thousand dollars a year; testifying before a Senate committee, Wallace put the 1944 gross sales at four million dollars;
even without his fifteen-thousand-dollar salary at *The New
Republic,* Wallace would be a rich man.

During the twenties, Wallace also occupied himself with
editing the family paper and with statistical work on price
fluctuations. In 1920 he published a technical book entitled

Agricultural Prices, and in 1923, in collaboration with E. N. Bressman, a textbook on *Corn and Corn Growing.* The family lost *Wallace's Farmer* in 1930, after an ill-advised expansion in 1929; Wallace was abroad at the time and cabled his objections, but too late. The paper went bankrupt and was bought by new owners, who retained Wallace as editor on a salary. In the 1932 presidential campaign, Wallace broke with family tradition to support Roosevelt —and, as it turned out, to begin his public career.

The depression that began in 1929 hit agriculture even harder than industry. The business prosperity of the twenties had not included the farmer; while industrial prices soared, farm prices recovered only moderately from the postwar depression. Thus the farmer was caught between the "scissors," selling his crop at low prices and buying manufactured goods at high prices. The 1929 collapse widened the scissors: industrial production was cut, but there was no way for millions of farmers to get together on production cuts; the result was that farm prices, set on the only free market left in the American economy, dropped even faster than industrial prices.

By the end of 1932, the farm crisis was as severe, though not so well publicized, as the banking crisis. In the rich farm states of Iowa, Kansas, and Wisconsin, farmers were going in for direct action: forcibly preventing foreclosure sales; threatening to hang judges; dumping milk on the highways. In the Northwest there was even talk of secession from the Union. Something drastic had to be done— but, as in the case of the banks, not too drastic. Just as the New Dealers closed the banks without taking advantage of the crisis to nationalize them, so they worked out a farm program which raised farm prices but reformed none of the social injustices within agriculture itself.

The New Deal farm program had only one aim: to raise farm prices. This could have been done, theoretically, either by enlarging the export market or by cutting production. The former method had been preferred by most farm leaders—including Wallace, Peek, and Wilson—throughout the twenties; they had supported the various McNary-Haughen bills passed by Congress and vetoed by Republican presidents. McNary-Haughenism was an imitation of industrial practice: just as the steel industry dumped its products abroad at cut prices, so farm products would be dumped abroad, with Government subsidies making up the difference in price to the farmer. By 1932, McNary-Haughenism was economically dead; the export market would not absorb American farm surpluses at any price. The New Dealers therefore copied another industrial technique—cutting production. Their program gave the Secretary of Agriculture authority to pay cash benefits to farmers who signed contracts agreeing to reduce their planted acreage, the money being raised by taxes levied on the processors of farm products.*

* They could not, however, resist making political capital out of Hoover's halfhearted efforts to restrict farm production. Wallace and George Peek wrote a campaign pamphlet aimed at the farmers, in which they indignantly charged: "The Republican Party and Mr. Hoover stand squarely . . . for restricting production to the demand of the domestic market, which is difficult in practice . . . and un-American in principle." [19] So, too, Roosevelt denounced Hoover's reckless Government spending and promised to balance the budget. A presidential campaign is indeed a strange and wonderful thing.

In his "farm speech" at Topeka, Kansas, that fall, Roosevelt outlined the program, with excellent political results. In March, 1933, Wallace's first act as Secretary of Agriculture was to call a conference of some fifty farm leaders and to get them to agree on the Agricultural Adjustment Act, based on the Topeka program. The farm lobby was powerful, the farm situation was urgent, and within two months A.A.A. had gone through Congress. The last great free-market sector of the American economy had come under State control.

THE SPLIT IN AGRICULTURE

In the volumes of the *Reader's Guide to Periodical Literature* covering the period 1925-1932 there are three entries under "Wallace, Henry Agard," all for technical papers in academic publications. In the single volume, 1933-1935, there is more than a solid column of articles by and about "Wallace, Henry Agard." This sudden rise to fame was somewhat accidental—or providential, as Wallace himself would probably say. Roosevelt's first choice for Agriculture was Tugwell, his second was Morgenthau; only when both had declined, did he fix on the Iowa farm editor.[20]

Wallace's first two years as Secretary of Agriculture were in many ways the most distinguished of his career; perhaps he himself was most satisfied and content then. He was fresh to national politics—an idealist of high intentions, with a scientifically trained mind and a thorough knowledge of agriculture. He seems to have impressed his subordinates in those days with his modesty, human decency, competence, energy, and receptivity to new ideas. Even a conservative newspaperman could say of him, retrospectively: "To have talked with Henry Wallace in 1933 was an inspiration." [21] And the atrabilious Frank R. Kent wrote in 1934 that Wallace was notable among the New Dealers for his "lack of cocksureness," adding: "He has no vestige of the infallibility complex . . . and does not attempt to cover up failure." [22] Last fall Kent wrote a bitter article in *The Saturday Evening Post* making just the opposite point about Wallace. It is not Kent, however, who has changed, but Wallace.

What happened to Wallace was very much like what happened to another nonpolitical, scientifically trained man of good intentions: Herbert Hoover. Wallace, like Hoover, found that clashes of interest do not yield to the engineering approach, and that something more than "objective analysis" of "the facts" is needed to solve the problems created by an inequitable economic system. Like Hoover, he came to grief because he lacked human and political imagination. The "purge" of the rebels in the Department of Agriculture, which came just two years after he took office, marked the end of Wallace as a fighter for the underdog. He has talked a good fight ever since, however.

Although A.A.A. did a fairly good job in increasing farm income—with the help of a couple of opportune droughts—it said nothing as to how this income was to be distributed. There were rich farmers and poor farmers: in 1929, almost eight million people lived on farms which yielded a *family* income of less than six hundred dollars a year, "based on value of products sold, traded or used." [23] There were also some three million wage-workers on farms, plus some thirteen million people in tenant families and another three million in sharecropping families. Since A.A.A.

benefits were paid to the owner of the land, they did not help the last three categories. The question of the consumer also arose, since A.A.A. failed to specify to what extent higher farm prices should come out of the middleman's and processor's profits and to what extent out of the consumer's pocket.

The new Secretary soon found himself in the middle of a conflict between the old-line farm leaders, who had traditionally dominated the policy of the Department, and a group of urban liberals brought in by the New Deal. The former were represented chiefly by the Farm Bureau Federation, the lobby of the top 25 per cent of the nation's farmers—the "four-hundred-acre farmers." They wanted no change in the status of their tenants or hired hands, and no redistribution of farm income. The food processors—packers, canners, millers, milk distributors—were closely allied with the farm leaders. George Peek, the businessman who served as the first A.A.A. administrator, put it in a sentence: "The sole aim and object of this act is to raise prices." This was true, historically. But a group in the Department felt that A.A.A. should go farther. Their leaders were Rexford Tugwell, the Under-Secretary of Agriculture, and Jerome Frank, who was General Counsel of the A.A.A. (and is now a Federal judge). Also prominent were Lee Pressman, of Frank's staff (now C.I.O. general counsel); Frederick C. Howe, a veteran reformer who headed the newly created Consumers' Council in the A.A.A.; and Gardner Jackson, who was Howe's aide. The rebels were concerned about A.A.A.'s effect on the agricultural underdog, and they worried when Justice Brandeis

predicted to Jackson—accurately enough, as it turned out—
that A.A.A. would speed up centralization of farm ownership and push still more tenants down into the status of
laborers. The old-line farm leaders worried not at all about
such matters. As Peek remarked, apropos of the rebels'
social conscience: "This is the Department of Agriculture,
not the Department of Everything."

There is no doubt that Wallace was worried, by social
conscience and, even more, by the existence of a conflict.
He supported the rebels, discreetly but sympathetically, except when the pressures became too strong. Then he re-
acted as he did when one of the rebels brought him a hor-
rifying report on conditions among farm laborers in the
Connecticut River Valley: *We can't touch that. It's dynamite!* * As indeed it was: the farm bloc was extremely
sensitive about "interference" on behalf of the hired man,
which is why Congress excluded farm labor from the scope
of the Wages and Hours law. But when the going was not
too tough, Wallace leaned toward the rebels. When Peek
brought his differences with Frank to a showdown at the
end of A.A.A.'s first year, Wallace accepted Peek's resignation. Characteristically, he then appointed Chester Davis,
who turned out to be a more suave (and more effective)
version of his predecessor. Also characteristically, he worked
closely with the Farm Bureau in administrative matters
even while he was backing the Bureau's opponents inside

---

* This is not a direct quotation; it is the recollection, 12 years later, of the
person to whom Wallace was talking. In preparing this book, I interviewed
a number of people who had been associated in one way or another with
Wallace. Their memories of what was said on various occasions are put
in italics, to indicate that they are to be taken as accurate in spirit but not
necessarily in literal text.

A.A.A.: the Bureau's eighteen hundred county agents also became the local A.A.A. agents, thus getting an inside track which caused a journalist to note later on: "Although the New Deal's lavish benefit payments helped all farm organizations, they helped the Farm Bureau the most." [24] The Wallaces themselves were "four-hundred-acre farmers," so perhaps it is surprising not that the Secretary in the end backed the Farm Bureau but rather that it took him two years to make up his mind to do so. Meanwhile, he exercised his talent for being on both sides of the fence simultaneously, as well as sitting on it. As George Peek, a blunt and simple man, reminisces, almost with admiration: "Secretary Wallace, who had an elastic mind capable of any stretching, alone managed to be in both groups." [25]

WALLACE AND THE SHARECROPPERS

The bitterest row was that over the sharecroppers. It gave Administrator Davis the opening he needed to purge the A.A.A. rebels. It involved both justice to the oppressed and political dynamite. And it repeatedly exposed the timidity and opportunism that canker Wallace's personality.

As everyone has known since 1934—and as practically no one knew before then—the millions of white and colored men, women, and children who raise most of the South's cotton on a "share-crop" basis, are the bottom stratum of American society. The Left-wing press used to call them "peasants," but the comparison was unfair—to the peasant. Few European peasants are as destitute as the sharecroppers. In 1933, a group led by H. L. Mitchell began to organize what later became the Southern Tenant Farmers Union—the first attempt to organize the sharecroppers.

Mitchell, a Socialist, got Norman Thomas to make a trip
through the South in 1934 and see things for himself. Ap-
palled, Thomas issued a detailed report which received
wide publicity. He also induced Dr. William Amberson,
of the University of Tennessee, to make a sociological study
of five hundred typical sharecropping families; Amberson
found, among other things, that the average *family* income
was $262 a year.[26]

The Thomas report charged that A.A.A. was making
things *worse* for the sharecroppers, since the landowners
naturally first withdrew from production those acres which
were being worked by tenants and sharecroppers. Thus tens
of thousands of sharecropping families not only got no
cash benefits from A.A.A. (since these were paid to the
owner) but also were pushed off the land into unemployment. Wallace's reactions were those of a Secretary of Agriculture rather than a Champion of the Common Man. He
issued a counter-statement accusing Thomas of exaggerat-
ing, for political purposes, the plight of the sharecroppers;
and he denied that A.A.A. was affecting them adversely.*
When Mitchell and Thomas tried, repeatedly, to get an appointment to see Wallace about the sharecroppers, the Secretary was somehow always busy or out of town. They
never did get in to see him.† They were, however, able to

* The following year, he backtracked. "We recognize," he told a Congressional committee on March 5, 1935, "that the A.A.A. cotton program has
probably added to the immediate difficulties of sharecroppers. . . . It is
inevitable in a period of emergency that such disturbances occur." Two
days later (March 7, 1935) he testified as to desirable amendments to A.A.A.
but proposed nothing to help the sharecroppers. Wallace is not the man to
fight against the inevitable (or even the probable).
† This glacial reception was mildly surprising to Thomas, who had met

see President Roosevelt twice in the same period—presumably because he was not so busy.

The reasons for Wallace's coyness were not obscure. Sharecropping was essential—or thought to be—to cotton; cotton was essential to the South; the Southern Democratic Congressmen were essential to Roosevelt. Tugwell, whom Thomas *was* able to see, asked him quite frankly: *What would YOU do if you had to keep on good terms with the Southern Congressmen?* And a revealing exchange took place during one of Thomas' interviews with the President. Showing Roosevelt a copy of the standard A.A.A. cotton contract (which had been drafted largely by Oscar Johnson, manager of the world's largest cotton plantation, the Delta farms), Thomas called his attention to its only safeguard for the sharecroppers: a clause, later "interpreted" into meaninglessness by Wallace, forbidding the landlord to evict tenants. *F.D.R.: That can mean something or nothing. THOMAS: It means nothing. F.D.R. (nettled): I'm a damn sight better politician than you are, Norman. THOMAS: That's obvious, since you are sitting behind that desk, and I'm in front of it. F.D.R.: What you don't understand is that a new breed of politicians is growing up in the South, and we must go slow on them.*

It seems not too wild a surmise that Wallace refused to see Thomas because he did not want to face the fact that

---

Wallace several times and had found him friendly and even cautiously interested in Socialist ideas. Wallace had, in fact, sent in a twenty-five dollar check to Thomas' 1932 campaign fund, thus boxing the political compass in true Wallacian style: a registered Republican, he gave money to the Socialists and voted with the Democrats.

the sharecroppers had to be sacrificed for political reasons. Tugwell and Roosevelt were more honest—or cynical—about it.

THE REAL FIGHT: MILK AND MEAT

The Tugwell-Frank group fought hard on the share-cropper issue, but they didn't get anywhere. Their position was weak because the interests of the sharecroppers—like those of the farm wage-workers, who didn't even get pub-licity out of A.A.A.—clashed with those of the powerful organized farmers. Wallace, therefore, resolutely stifled the sympathies which the sharecroppers, as the commonest of Common Men, no doubt aroused in him.

In dealing with the food-processing interests, however, the rebels had a much stronger tactical position, since here the enemy was not The Farmer (who is Good in our political ideology) but Big Business (which is Bad). They also had the advantage of Wallace's undercover support: as a Midwest farm leader, Wallace, like his Republican father and grandfather, was as instinctively against "the monopolies" as he was instinctively for "the farmer."

The main struggle was over opening the books of the food processors. The contracts they signed with A.A.A. al-lowed them to get together to fix prices without laying themselves open to prosecution under the antitrust laws; in return for this considerable concession, A.A.A. stipulated that (a) the consumer should get some consideration; and (b) the farmers should get some benefit from any price in-crease—in short, that fixed prices should not result simply in bigger profits. Clearly, as Roosevelt had remarked about the cotton contract, such stipulations could mean something or nothing, depending on how the contracts were actually administered. A "friendly" administration would mean that the A.A.A. contracts would be merely a means of rigging prices to mulct the consumer, as was the case with most of the N.R.A. codes. General Counsel Frank was not "friendly": he insisted that every contract include a clause giving the A.A.A. the right to inspect the books of the company so as to see just what the higher prices meant to the farmer and the consumer. Wallace supported this view by ordering that no contract was to be signed until it had been approved by Frank's office. The food companies resented this provision as Un-American and Unconstitutional—also for more serious unexpressed reasons—nor were they placated when Frank pointed out that they were not obliged to sign an A.A.A. contract unless they wanted to. The farm organizations, which had long worked amicably with the food interests, went along with them on this issue, as did Administrator Davis of A.A.A. The rebels were closely allied with the veteran reformer, Frederick C. Howe, and the Consumers' Council he headed inside the A.A.A. "With the pressures of both camps upon him," writes Wallace's personal bard, Russell Lord, "Wallace fell silent and uncommunicative. A lion for principle, he would not or could not bring himself at the time, it seemed, to enter into differences when differences became personal. He hated quarreling; it literally made him sick. So he sat silent, and seemed for weeks on end at this critical juncture inept, irresolute, helpless." [27] This interpretation is nonsense—the differences were not personal but principled—but the picture of Wallace's reactions to any kind of a struggle is accurate. Wallace wants two things above all others: to be friends with everyone, and to win. In a fight, you make enemies and you may lose.

THE GREAT PURGE

The conflict ended abruptly on February 5, 1935. That morning the leading rebels—including Frank, Jackson, Howe, and Pressman—found on their desks when they arrived for work a note from Chester Davis requesting their resignations "forthwith." There had been no warning at all; in fact, just a few days earlier, the rebels had won a victory over Davis, with Wallace's aid, in the matter of opening the books of the canned asparagus industry. Except for the cynical Pressman, they were all convinced that Davis had acted without Wallace's knowledge and that once "H.A." heard about it he would discipline Davis. Gardner Jackson, in particular, should have recalled Wallace's reaction a few months earlier when he had told him about a secret meeting of the milk interests in Philadelphia to plan how to force the rebels out of the Department. Wallace had shown no moral indignation, no ardor for great principles, but had ruminated with cool detachment: *You know, Pat, I can't understand you. You always want to act when you see something wrong. I don't. I want to sit under a tree. The cycle of time brings all things . . . I'm in an impossible situation here; the pressures are great; I think I'll have to drop either Davis or Frank.*

In actuality, not only had Davis acted with Wallace's approval, but Wallace, as he himself told the press two days later, had secretly agreed to drop the rebels two months earlier. A good excuse was needed. Davis found it in a legal interpretation of the cotton contract which

Frank's office had put out; the interpretation limited the right of the owner to dispossess his sharecroppers. Davis convinced Wallace that the interpretation was not only incorrect but was a deliberate attempt to put over "a fast one"; he demanded that Wallace choose between him and the Frank group; this time Wallace chose Davis. The coup was shrewdly timed to take place while Under-Secretary Tugwell, who had used his influence with Roosevelt to protect the rebels, was in Florida on vacation. By the time he heard about it and rushed back to Washington to protest, it was a *fait accompli*.

The purgees tried all day to see Wallace, who, as is his wont at unpleasant moments, was just not around. Finally, late in the afternoon, word came that he would see two of them. Frank and one other went into his office. *WALLACE: Jerome, you've been the best fighter I've had for my ideas, but I've had to fire you. The farm people are just too strong. I've got to go along and you've got to go. FRANK: All right, it's your choice and you have to make it yourself. I understand. But why not at least tell us about it? Why let us hear about it first from Davis? WALLACE: I just couldn't face you. FRANK: Will you let me hold up my resignation two or three days? There are some lawyers I brought into the division and they have families and I want a few days to get them jobs in other agencies. WALLACE: That sounds reasonable. I'll talk to Chester about it.* He went off to talk to Chester and didn't come back. After waiting in his office until seven, the other two went home.

The next day the papers carried the story. *The New York Times* quoted "Department officials" as predicting an end to " 'business-baiting' and sharp criticism of middle-man practices which Mr. Davis had always regarded as unwarranted." Unidentified "spokesmen for Secretary Wallace and Mr. Davis" charged that "those who resigned were troublemakers who let their social theories stand in the way of restoring farm prosperity." On February 7, Wallace held a press conference; he was uneasy, haggard, on the defensive, the picture of a guilt-ridden man. He evaded all questions as to the reasons for the purge, saying only that it had been undertaken "in the interests of the greatest possible harmony." REPORTER: "The rightwingers were ousted last year and now the leftwingers are going. Where is the boat headed for?" WALLACE: "You can't have the ship listing right and then left. . . . It must go straight down the middle of the road."

The chief victims of the purge were the sharecroppers. The clause of the cotton contract in dispute between Frank and Davis-Wallace was Section 7, which provided that the landlord "shall permit all tenants to continue in the occupancy of their houses on this farm, rent free, for the years 1934 and 1935." The Southern Tenant Farmers Union kept complaining to A.A.A. that its members were being evicted anyway. When five hundred such cases had piled up, Davis was forced to send down to Arkansas an official investigator, Mrs. Mary Conner Myers. After a three-week investigation, Mrs. Myers filed a report showing that conditions were even worse than the S.T.F.U. had claimed. The report was shown to Senator Joe Robinson, who happened to be (a) from Arkansas and (b) the Democratic majority leader. Joe didn't think much of the report, and it was never made public. Frank, on the contrary, was impressed by the report and even went so far as to interpret Section 7 to mean what it said: that tenants could not be evicted. This was the "fast interpretation" that Davis and Wallace used as an excuse for the purge. Soon afterward, Wallace gave out *his* interpretation of Section 7: that it meant only that the same number of tenants must be housed, not that *any particular family* had a right to stay on its farm! The Arkansas Supreme Court thought highly of Henry's interpretation and used it as a basis for throwing out all the eviction cases the S.T.F.U. had brought before it, after which a reign of terror began in the countryside. S.T.F.U. families were forcibly evicted, their houses shot up, and their men beaten and killed by vigilante gangs.[28]

The purge also resulted in the reduction of the A.A.A. Consumer's Council to a research agency, thus removing its power to annoy the packers and canners. One may imagine the crisis of conscience Wallace went through in those days: by family tradition and personal conviction he was the foe of big business—no theme is harped on more constantly in all his writings, indeed, from the beginning up to the present, than the evils of monopoly—and yet here he was giving the victory to the forces of Satan inside his own Department. A few days after the purge, he arranged an accidental meeting with Frank at Tugwell's apartment. Awkwardly, after much embarrassment, he admitted he felt badly about the whole affair and asked whether Frank would be willing to return to the Department as Solicitor, a higher post than A.A.A. Counsel but one safely removed from the battle-line. Not much attracted to the job, Frank said he would think it over; Wallace, however, must have "talked to Chester," for the offer was never formally made. A year later, the two men met again; Wallace, who by that time had concluded that he had been entirely wrong to go along with Davis' coup, told Frank that he had burned his diary for the period and that he never wanted to think about it again. Thus the rebels may be said to have scored a "moral victory." Their opponents were no doubt quite satisfied with the extremely material-istic victory they had won.

THE SOCIAL EFFECTS OF A.A.A.

According to the Wallace legend, the seven years in Agriculture were years of (a) progressive reform and (b) successful stabilization of the farm economy. Both claims are . . . legendary.

We have just examined Wallace's behavior as to (a) in the crucial 1933–1935 period. It is true that later on the Department paid some attention to the agricultural under-privileged. But this was due not to Wallace but to Tugwell. After the 1935 purge, Tugwell was able to get a consolation prize from Roosevelt, who gave him authority to set up an agency, with an initial budget of four hundred million dollars and fifteen thousand employees, to finance the re-moval of low-income farmers and sharecroppers onto sub-sistence homesteads on good land. This project, conceived by Tugwell and Harry Hopkins, was called the Rural Re-settlement Administration; it later became the Farm Se-curity Administration and is now called the Farmers' Home Administration. Rural Resettlement aroused so little enthusiasm in Wallace that it was forced to begin life in the more sympathetic atmosphere of Ickes' Department of the Interior.[29] Later on, after the politically unpopular Tugwell had been forced out of the Government service, Wallace consented to permit Resettlement to migrate to his own Department, where, it is only fair to state, he became more friendly, appointing liberals to head it.

Rural Resettlement was essentially social work and had no more profound effect on the evils it combated than social work generally has. A.A.A. was the significant part of the New Deal farm program, and its effects turned out to be just about what Brandeis and the rebels had predicted they would be. "This increased income," wrote the editors of the London *Economist* in 1937, "does not seem to have been very equally distributed among the different classes of people dependent upon it. Thus while net cash income in farming increased between 1933 and 1935 by 40 per cent, the amount paid in wages to farm laborers increased by only about 14 per cent. Tenant farmers, especially the sharecroppers, also do not seem to have received their fair share." [30] And a study made in 1937 by the Department of Agriculture itself showed that if under A.A.A. the rich got richer, the rest of the song also applied: the poor got poorer. The percentage of farm acreage operated by tenants increased from 29 per cent in 1929 to 32 per cent in 1935; between 1930 and 1935, sixty thousand more sharecroppers and two hundred thousand more tenants appeared. "It is a conservative estimate," concludes this report made after four years of A.A.A., "that one-third of the farm families of the nation are living on standards of living so low as to make them slum families." [31]

THE ECONOMIC EFFECTS OF A.A.A.

What of part (b) of the Wallace legend: that his farm program saved agriculture from economic disaster? Farm income did increase greatly between 1933 and 1936, an increase in which A.A.A. undoubtedly played a part. The improvement was effected at the expense of the consumer: A.A.A. was business sabotage according to the Veblenian formula. Wallace had written quite frankly as early as 1920 that, if other ways of getting higher prices failed, farmers should "sabotage" their product "in the same heartless, efficient way as labor and capital" so that the latter "will be forced to come to an agreement with farmers on production and price matters." This sabotage was greatly helped along by severe nation-wide droughts in 1934 and 1936. "By the combined efforts of man and nature," wrote Wallace after the 1934 drought, "the domestic wheat surplus was nearly wiped out, hog supplies were brought down . . . and corn supplies promised to be reduced." [32] (One recalls the quip of Benjamin Stolberg in his *Economic Consequences of the New Deal*: "There is nothing the New Deal has so far done that could not have been done better by an earthquake.") How successful A.A.A. would have been without divine intervention is hard to say. Farm exports declined between 1932 and 1935. And the farmers to some extent got around A.A.A. by more intensive cultivation of the remaining acres; thus, although the cotton growers got one hundred million dollars in benefits for withdrawing ten million acres from production, they farmed the rest so energetically that the 1933 crop was actually bigger than 1932.

When the Supreme Court invalidated A.A.A. in 1936, Wallace evolved his most celebrated farm policy: the "ever-normal granary." Wallace got the idea from reading a thesis by a Chinese student at Columbia on "The Economic Principles of Confucius"; there was also some resemblance to Joseph's farm policy in ancient Egypt. The program looked reasonable enough on paper: in good harvest years, the Government keeps up prices by buying surplus crops, which it stores; in bad years, it sells the stored crops. Thus the farmer is protected from market fluctuations and the consumer gets an even flow of farm products. However, neither Confucius nor Joseph had to worry about the capitalist market. What happened was that the farmers, assured of good prices, produced so much that by 1939 the Government's stocks of wheat, cotton, and other farm products were so huge as to cause a storage problem—to say nothing of the vast sums of Government money tied up in the stored crops; nor was it clear how these surpluses were ever to be sold without breaking the market. In August, 1938, Wallace admitted that the wheat farmers faced catastrophe, with the second largest harvest on record coming in on top of the record carry-over from previous crops. He announced a plan for subsidizing the export of one hundred million bushels of wheat, i.e., dumping them on the world market at an expected loss of twenty-five million dollars. The Department of Agriculture asked the farmers to reduce their wheat planting from eighty million acres to fifty-five million; even so, a record four-hundred-million-bushel surplus was expected by the end of 1939. The Ever-Normal Granary was becoming the Ever-Abnormal Granary.

The liberal historian, Louis Hacker, wrote sadly in 1938: "On the basis of the experiences in agriculture, it was possible to say that the New Deal was producing dislocations every whit as profound as those iniquities it was succeeding in redressing." [33] The war, of course, saved the situation by creating a big demand for farm products—whereupon the size of the stored-up surpluses became a proof of Wallace's foresight!

3. Prophet of the People's Century (1941–1946)

I N THE SUMMER of 1940, the Democratic convention, under pressure from Roosevelt, nominated Henry Wallace for Vice-President. Roosevelt's insistence on Wallace for his running-mate is one more indication of his political insight. A better choice could hardly have been made.

"The Vice-President of the United States," Tom Marshall once observed, "is like a man in a cataleptic state: he cannot speak; he cannot move; he suffers no pain; and yet he is perfectly conscious of everything that is going on about him." Wallace's incumbency, however, gave the lie to this epigram: he spoke and moved freely, and he was, as usual, only imperfectly conscious of what went on about him.

No Vice-President has played so important a role: he threw himself into the crusade for democracy with an ardor that made Winston Churchill seem a Quisling. Not only did he occupy important posts in the warmaking apparatus, but, above all, he became the country's outstanding moral apologist for the conflict. The role Wilson played in the first war was assumed by Wallace in the second. After the early Atlantic-Charter-Four-Freedoms period, Roosevelt lost interest in noble war aims and made no secret of his growing "realism." He must have often congratulated himself on his choice of Wallace, who never lost heart and produced ardent moral rhetoric to the very end.

Just as it is generally believed that Wallace, as Secretary of Agriculture, pursued liberal policies, so is it widely believed that he is a "global democrat" of long standing. Actually, the second belief has as little foundation as we have already seen the first to have. Both are part of that mythology which grows so luxuriantly about his figure. Up to the year 1941, Wallace's concern with global matters was confined to the increase of agricultural exports; his internationalism went no farther than supporting Hull's reciprocal trade treaties. In the "collective security" debate, he was definitely on the isolationist side, as his midwestern farm background might have led one to anticipate.* Even the outbreak of the war made no change in Wallace's ideas; his 1940 book, *The American Choice,* proposed hemispheric isolation as the method of meeting the German war menace.

In 1941 Germany invaded Russia and Japan attacked Pearl Harbor. Bellicose internationalism became expedient for an American leader who was just beginning his association with the Stalinoid Left. A profound change occurred: from an agrarian politician, Wallace became the Conscience of the World (freedom-loving areas, that is); from a perplexed administrator, he became the Friend of

* Henry's only recorded reaction to Munich, reproduced *in toto* from *The New York Times* of October 2, 1938: "St. Louis, October 1: Secretary of Agriculture Henry A. Wallace said today that assurance of European peace constituted 'a blessing' to the American farmer, who pays for temporary war prosperity twice over in maladjustments after the war."

the Common Man and the Prophet of the People's Century. After 1941 Wallace's rhetoric soared unhampered by niggling problems like sharecropping. The world is wide, and the Common Man is everywhere—and nowhere. After 1941, Wallace's real deterioration began, when he took the whole world for his benevolent province, losing whatever contact with reality he had had up to then and becoming more and more an oratorical gasbag, a great wind of rhetoric blowing along the prevailing trade route of Stalinoid liberalism.

THE "FREE WORLD" SPEECH

Wallace's most celebrated wartime oration, an effort he never surpassed and one which made him overnight into the spokesman for "the people's century," was the speech he delivered to the Free World Association in New York City on May 8, 1942. Political speeches do not withstand the passage of time very well, but few have dated so rapidly in five years. Rereading it today, with the outlines of the postwar-prewar world taking grim shape about us, is a peculiar experience. One wonders about the psychology of the speaker and of the many educated, idealistic citizens who mistook for reality a hallucinatory vision.

"This is a fight between a free world and a slave world," Wallace began in clarion tones. "Just as the United States in 1862 could not remain half slave and half free, so in 1942 the world must make its decision for a complete victory one way or the other.

"As we begin the final stages of this fight to the death . . . it is worth while to refresh our minds about the march of freedom for the common man. The idea of freedom—

the freedom that we in the United States know and love
so well—is derived from the Bible with its extraordinary
emphasis on the dignity of the individual. Democracy is
the only true political expression of Christianity. . . .

"The people are on the march toward even fuller freedom than the most fortunate peoples of the world have
hitherto enjoyed. No Nazi counter-revolutionist will stop
it. . . . The people's revolution is on the march, and the
devil and all his angels cannot prevail against it. They cannot prevail, for on the side of the people is the Lord."

This encouraging view of the future, long since
punctured by postwar events, was possible to Wallace because his is a Victorian optimism of progress, based on a
belief in the automatic beneficence of industrialization plus
popular education: "Down the years, the people of the
United States have moved steadily forward in the practice
of democracy. Through universal education, they can now
read and write and form opinions of their own. . . . Everywhere, reading and writing are accompanied by industrial
progress, and industrial progress sooner or later brings a
strong labor movement."

That universal literacy, with all media of communication in the hands of the dominant class—whether the
Soviet politburo or our own hucksters—has become a
means of *preventing* people from having "opinions of their
own"—this is no clearer to Wallace today than it was to
Herbert Spencer in the last century. Nor is there any place
in his antiquated cosmology for the two great historical de-
velopments of our time: the degeneration of the Russian
Revolution and the growth of Nazism. For the industrialization of Russia and the well-publicized reduction of il-

literacy by the Soviet regime have been accompanied by a *contraction* of the area of political freedom; while Hitler came to power precisely in that European country which was most heavily industrialized and had the finest system of public education, as well as the strongest labor move-ment. Wallace attempted to meet these objections by as-serting (1) that "in the process" of abolishing illiteracy "Russia's appreciation of freedom was tremendously in-creased," which simply is not true (unless in the sense that one values what one hasn't got); and (2) that Germany lacks a tradition of self-government, which merely raises the question as to why so industrialized and well-educated a nation failed to develop a democratic tradition.

If such phenomena simply refused to fit into Wallace's historical scheme, so did the fact that for the second time in a generation the world was at war. The sins of capital-ism he loaded onto the scapegoat Hitler, "the curse of the modern world," much as Hitler loaded them onto the Jews. Instead of seeing Hitlerism as the terrible result of the decadence of both capitalism and the 1917 Revolution, Wallace presented it as a monstrosity which in some way had arisen entirely outside history—a kind of pure diab-olism. The speech referred to Hitler as "Satan" no fewer than seven times.

Against the black picture of Satan-Hitler, Wallace set a bright lantern-slide of the situation on the Anglo-American-Russian side of the battle-lines: a steady, inevitable for-ward-march by the common people toward ever-increasing democracy and security: "The march of freedom of the past 150 years has been a long-drawn-out people's revolu-tion. . . . The people's revolution aims at peace and not at violence, but if the rights of the common man are attacked, it unleashes the ferocity of a she-bear who has lost a cub. . . . The people, in their millennial and revolutionary march toward manifesting here on earth the dignity that is in every human soul, hold as their credo the Four Freedoms enunciated by President Roosevelt. These Four Freedoms are the very core of the revolution for which the United Nations have taken their stand." It was characteristic of Wallace that an advertising slogan like the Four Freedoms (*Love Those Freedoms!*), which are now as mercifully forgotten as Phoebe Snow and the Sapolio jingles, should have appeared to him as the "core" of a "people's revolution." Also characteristic was the notion of a revolution whose Navy was commanded by a Knox, whose Army was led by a Stimson, and whose foreign policy was conducted by a Hull.

On this shaky ideological foundation, Wallace reared a shining dream palace of freedom and plenty for all. He quoted his "half-serious" remark to Madame Litvinoff, the wife of the Russian diplomat: "The object of this war is to make sure that everybody in the world has the privilege of drinking a quart of milk a day." ("Yes, even a pint," cautiously amends the Soviet lady.) Or, in more grandiose terms:

"The people are on the march toward even fuller freedom than the most fortunate peoples of the world have hitherto enjoyed. . . . The peace must mean a better standard of living for the common man, not merely in the United States and England, but also in Germany, Italy and Japan. . . . Those who write the peace must think of

the whole world. There can be no privileged peoples. . . .
Some have spoken of the American Century. I say that the
century on which we are entering—the century that will
come out of this war—can be and must be the century of
the common man."

A joke is now going the rounds in Germany. Two
friends are discussing the possibility of a third world war.
"Do you think we will survive it?" asks one. "That doesn't
worry me so much," replies the other. "But I'm wondering
if we'll survive the next peace."

Wallese has seldom reached more pathological extremes
than in the "Free World" speech. Its emotional appeal lay
in the combination of two very deep and mutually exclusive American folk-ideologies: camp-meeting revivalism
and optimism about scientific progress. It also combined
provincialism and internationalism in a bewildering way.
Like Willkie, whose *One World* a year later sold over a
million copies in the first two weeks of publication, Wallace emerges as a latter-day American type: the Global
Backwoodsman. It is perhaps superfluous to add that, in
his speech, Wallace included Russia among the freedom-
loving democracies, a historical insight that would hardly
have occurred to him before June 22, 1941.

Soon Wallace was spinning all sorts of global fantasies.
An International Investment Corporation to reshape the
face of the earth in the image of T.V.A. An International
Air Authority ("The air space above this earth must be
used to serve the needs of trade and travel for the Common Man."). An International Police Force. In high Wallesian style, he proposed to keep the peace by "bombing
mercilessly" recalcitrant nations.[34]

THE CHOSEN PEOPLE

In the "Free World" speech, Wallace counterposes to Henry Luce's frankly chauvinist "American Century" the notion of "The People's Century." Yet, as we have pointed out, there are intimations here and there that perhaps the two concepts are not so far apart as might appear. Certainly Wallace makes no effort to hide his admiration for his native land; if he has some kind words for other nations, it is always because they are toiling upward to the high culture that the U.S.A. has already achieved. In the past, Wallace had struck the jingoistic note with naïve frankness. In 1938, he had, on one occasion, summoned "all classes to cooperate together to make this land truly the Chosen Land of the Lord, an example and a help to other lands." [35] And, on another, he had written: "For the first time in the history of the world, we have here in the United States the possibility of combining into a truly harmonious whole all the pre-requisites to the good life. . . . Other nations may rival us in one or two of these progressive forces, but not a single nation is so universally blessed." [36] And in 1940, he had carefully listed the ways in which America is superior to Europe:

(a) "We have not yet become slaves to national hates."

(b) "We can never feel at home again in the midst of diplomatic intrigue of the sort which seems always under way in the Old World."

(c) "We do not consider ourselves a part of the system of economic imperialism which dominates Europe and Africa and Asia."

(d) "We have no urge to take either markets or resources from other peoples by force."

(e) We are against "the dictator system," destruction, and soil erosion.

Conclusion: "So we are disillusioned with the Old World." However: "In saying this, we are not self-righteous." [37]

A month after the "Free World" speech, Wallace showed that his newly acquired internationalism had not changed his ideas about the Chosen Land. He joined hands with Luce, and indeed went him one better, in a speech delivered before a religious group on June 9, 1942, to which he gave the intriguing title: "Why Did God Make America?" This speech deserves to be better known than it is. "History thus far," Wallace begins, "seems to be but the prelude to a magnificent world symphony. In this prelude, many themes were played. One glorious theme is how the Lord God Jehovah had a special interest in one chosen race, the Jews, and in one promised land, Palestine. . . . But the Jews by themselves and Palestine by herself could not build the Kingdom of Heaven here on earth. The spiritual essence of Judaism would eventually find its expression here in America. But God held America back, and the Romans destroyed the Jewish nation." The divine election next seemed to descend on Rome, but God still held America back. In time, the British Empire arose, but "God still held his hand over America." Finally, like a football coach who reserves his star player for the crucial touchdown in the last quarter, God has given the signal to America, "the heir of the religious concepts of Palestine and the culture of Rome and England." The prelude to the world symphony is finished, and the magnificent opening chords of the major theme are heard. America is about to undertake God's mission of "building in the full sun of a new day for a peace which is not based on imperialistic intervention." Aware of her Manifest Destiny, she is taking up the White Man's Burden. The *Pax Americana* is to embrace the world.* "The American peace will be the peace of the common man."

SPAB, BEW, AND POW!

Apocalyptic speeches were not Wallace's only contribution to the war effort. He also held high executive posts in the wartime economic machinery. In August, 1941, Roosevelt put him at the head of a new top economic "coordinating" agency, the Supply Priorities and Allocations Board (S.P.A.B.), which folded six months later after no more and no less ineffectual an existence than its predecessors had had. As a consolation prize Roosevelt gave Wallace the Board of Economic Warfare (B.E.W.), an agency concerned with buying war supplies in foreign countries. At the beginning of 1942, Wallace was made chairman of B.E.W.; he appointed his close friend, Milo Perkins, Executive Director. Perkins, who originated the Food Stamp Plan, one of the few politically progressive and economically sensible innovations of the New Deal, was an able executive.

The main function of B.E.W. was to build up stockpiles of scarce raw materials: tin, rubber, quinine, etc. Wallace and

* Revised as of September, 1946, to exclude areas now enjoying the *Pax Sovietica.*

Perkins went at this aggressively; they also tried to use these big purchases to raise the living standards of the supplying countries. (This is one of the rare instances of Wallace's actually trying to *do* something to implement his ideology.) Their freehanded spending brought them into conflict with Jesse Jones, of the R.F.C., who had authority to release or withhold funds for B.E.W.'s purchases. Their liberal social policy caused friction with the State Department—Cordell Hull and Will Clayton were the chief antagonists here—as in the case of B.E.W.'s unsuccessful attempt to insert into its Bolivian tin contracts clauses forcing the owners to spend some of their increased revenues on raising wages. Roosevelt finally settled the issue in April, 1942, in B.E.W.'s favor, taking away both Hull's political and Jones's financial veto powers. Or, rather, appeared to settle it. Actually, Hull secured a quiet reversal of the decision a month or two later on; while Jones, whose approach to the problems of war economy was that of a small-town banker, continued to hamper B.E.W. administratively and began to work on Congress to undermine Wallace and Perkins.*

By the spring of 1943, Jones was asking a Congressional committee to restore his former veto power over the B.E.W.'s purchases; since Jones was extremely, and indeed excessively, popular with Congress, there was a good chance that this might be done. Bernard Baruch, oddly enough, supported Wallace in the row; but Roosevelt preserved a discreet impartiality. Finally, in June, Wallace and Per-

---

* The classic Jones wartime story is his retort to a colleague who was groaning because one fifth of the entire stockpile of rubber had just been destroyed in a dock fire: "But the stuff's insured!"

kins were goaded into issuing a detailed public statement showing that B.E.W.'s record in amassing stockpiles was much better than R.F.C.'s had been. Jones replied in kind, less convincingly. The Wallace-Perkins idea was to compensate for Jones's inside track with Congress by an appeal to public opinion, thus putting pressure also on Roosevelt. The strategy misfired, however, and Wallace sustained the most unexpected and terrible blow of his whole career. Roosevelt took a "plague on both your houses" stand, rebuking both Jones and Wallace for making their quarrel public. But, as in the similar stand he took in the 1937 Little Steel Strike, the weight of Roosevelt's displeasure fell almost wholly on the Left: Wallace was abruptly kicked out of B.E.W., which was handed over to the Jones crowd, in the person of Leo Crowley, the sixty-thousand-dollar-a-year head of Standard Gas and Electric Corporation. *The New Republic* editorialized, with little exaggeration, that Roosevelt's action was "the most severe shock to his liberal followers since he has been in office"—except for his aid to Franco during the Spanish Civil War. The government agencies "in which New Deal ways of thinking prevailed" had already been reduced to two: the B.E.W. and the Federal Communications Commission; now only one was left. Fighting a modern war just doesn't seem to jibe with New Dealism. (This last conclusion is mine, not theirs.)

"HENRY . . . WOULD REMAIN LOYAL"

There is no recorded case of Henry Wallace's separating himself, on an issue of principle, either from power or from those who dispense it. So was it now. His reaction to Roosevelt's stab-in-the-back was not to resign the Vice-Presidency, not to protest Roosevelt's increasingly frank abandonment of New Deal principles, but to set off at once on a speaking tour in which he preached the pure New Deal gospel— and hailed Franklin D. Roosevelt as its chief prophet. "I have known the President intimately for ten years," he began his first speech, on July 26, before a large C.I.O. audience in Detroit, "and in the final showdown he has always put human rights first. There are powerful groups who hope to take advantage of the President's concentration on the war effort to destroy everything he has accomplished on the domestic front." His original idea had been to pay even more fulsome tribute to the man who had just thrown him to the wolves; friends persuaded him to tone it down. As Tugwell has noted, with perhaps a touch of malice, apropos of the B.E.W. episode: "The President . . . knew that however he was treated, Henry Wallace would remain loyal." [38]

With a demagogy bordering on the cynical, Wallace at Detroit went on to criticize not Roosevelt but "certain American fascists," who he inferred were typical of the business community, adding: "The reason Mr. Roosevelt is so hated by many big businessmen is the fact that he stopped making Washington a way station on the road to Wall Street." So extreme were his attacks on businessmen in this and later speeches that strong criticism was aroused. So on August 19, Henry took it back, explaining that fascist-minded businessmen were "a small minority" and that "perhaps 95 per cent or even 99 per cent do not fall into that category." He specifically exempted from his criticisms the small businessmen, who in Germany had furnished Hitler his most enthusiastic followers, because in American politics little business is Good and big business is Bad.

The situation was extremely complex. Roosevelt had unceremoniously kicked out Wallace after he had come into conflict with the reactionary Jesse Jones; he had done this despite the fact that Wallace's B.E.W., as even conservative observers admitted, was doing a much better job of economic warfare than Jones's R.F.C.; his motive for getting rid of Wallace must, therefore, have been political—i.e., that Wallace was the last of the unreconstructed New Dealers in high office. Shortly afterward, Roosevelt crossed the t's and dotted the i's when he said that "Dr. New Deal" was dead and had been replaced by "Dr. Win the War." Yet this was the man whom Wallace, immediately after his expulsion from B.E.W., toured the country to praise as the great leader and defender of . . . the New Deal. A month after Roosevelt had officially pronounced the New Deal dead, Wallace addressed the Democratic National Committee:

"One man more than any other in all history has given dynamic power and economic expression to the New Deal. That man is Roosevelt. Roosevelt has never denied the principles of the New Deal and he never will. They are a part of his very being. Roosevelt, God willing, will in the future give the New Deal a firmer foundation than it has ever had before. So, on with the New Deal, on with winning the war and forward march for peace, justice and jobs!" [39]

What the Democratic National Committee thought of this oration is not recorded. The more naïve of them may have had a slight feeling of dizziness. But the sophisticated must have reflected that only good could come from a free-wheeling prophet, safely removed from all posts of power, who was out to convince labor and the liberals that Roosevelt was still Their Leader. The strategy, into which Wallace—doubtless, as always, unconsciously—fitted smoothly, was simply the old political practice of working both sides of the street.

THE 1944 DEFEAT

The man "who has always put human rights first" had something even worse in store for the faithful Henry than the B.E.W. humiliation. Just a year later came the great vice-presidential doublecross. In the spring of 1944, Roosevelt sent Wallace on a "goodwill" tour of Siberia and China. Wallace accomplished the task successfully, telling the forced-labor deportees of Soviet Asia how inspiring it was to look into the open faces of free pioneers, observing in Chungking that "China today is guided by the mature wisdom of President Chiang," and expressing a (mimeographed) hope that the Sino-Soviet border would in future be as peaceful as the United States-Canadian boundary. In July, he got back to Washington, where he at once discovered that Roosevelt was not enthusiastic about his renomination for the vice-presidency. After Ickes, Rosenman, and finally Roosevelt himself had seen Wallace and tried tactfully to suggest that he withdraw—efforts which were frustrated by Wallace with gentle obtuseness—Roosevelt agreed to write a letter endorsing him for the renomination.

What happened at the Convention is well known: how both Byrnes and Wallace arrived there confident they had

Roosevelt's backing, how the liberal bloc made Roosevelt abandon Byrnes only to discover that the precious letter backing Wallace was a weasel-worded document which avoided the kind of commitment Roosevelt had made in 1940, how the big-city bosses plus the Southern delegates were able to beat Wallace with Truman (who also had a letter of endorsement from Roosevelt). Even this Roosevelt-engineered fiasco did not shake Wallace's peculiar devotion to his Leader (who also happened to be still the most powerful political boss of the liberal-labor forces Wallace hoped some day to lead). "The President did all I expected him to," he said bravely. "I told him that in justice to himself and myself there should be nothing in the nature of dictation." (In 1940, Roosevelt had flatly told the Convention that he would accept the nomination only if Wallace was his running-mate.) In a characteristic burst of euphoria, he even saw his defeat as providential: "I feel free now. If I were a candidate, I would have to follow a schedule and deal with issues from a partisan standpoint. This way, I can do more for liberalism."

His way of doing more for liberalism was to campaign ardently for the man who had knifed him because of his liberalism ("Wallace seems to us the superlatively good sport of all time," editorialized *The New Republic*). In his 1944 campaign speeches, as in those of 1940, Wallace resorted to a crude demagogy which, in a politician less obviously the friend of the Common Man, would remind one of Hitler. His theme was simple: a Republican victory is a Nazi victory. In 1940, he tied the Republicans "objectively" to Hitler and declared that opposition to Roosevelt, "whatever the motive," could only "play into the hands of Hitler" since he was "the man Hitler wants to see defeated." Hence: "I want to emphasize that replacement of Mr. Roosevelt, even if it were by the most patriotic leadership that could be found, would cause Hitler to rejoice." [40] In 1944, he continued in the same vein, insisting that the only people who opposed Roosevelt were "Germans, Japs and certain American troglodytes," and warning: "A Dewey victory, no matter how estimable Mr. Dewey himself may be personally, will inevitably give hope to the wrong element in Germany and Japan." [41] It is ironical that Wallace's own recent speeches abroad have now given the Republicans an opening—and a more legitimate one—for smearing *him* as the agent of a hostile foreign power.

SECRETARY OF COMMERCE

After the campaign, Roosevelt rewarded Wallace for his "good sportsmanship" by offering him any cabinet post he wanted *except* the one he really wanted, that of Secretary of State. Wallace chose Commerce, partly because the job carried with it control of the enormously powerful Federal Loan Agency, which had an authorized spending power of fourteen billion dollars and which included the Reconstruction Finance Corporation and a dozen other huge Government corporations; and partly because, for personal and political reasons, he wanted to oust the incumbent, his old enemy Jesse Jones. It does not seem to have occurred to Wallace that there was about as much chance of Congress' confirming his appointment to a post of such power as of Jesse Jones being offered the editorship of *The New Republic*. A bill was immediately introduced into the Senate taking

F.L.A. out of the jurisdiction of the Secretary of Commerce. Jones and Wallace both testified at the hearings on the bill; there was never the slightest doubt as to the attitude of the great majority of Senators toward their respective economic philosophies, or as to the outcome of the conflict.

Jones gave a classic description of F.L.A. and of his own credo:

"It is bigger than General Motors and General Electric and Montgomery Ward and everything else put together and you don't hear much about it because it is being run by businessmen, by men experienced in business, by men who haven't any ideas about remaking the world. (*Laughter and Applause*.) Plodders—not smart, just plodders, trying to do a job honestly and constructively. . . ."

"Have you ever used your powers," asked Senator Bailey, "for the purpose of determining the economic character or the social character of this country?" "I certainly have not," replied Jones. "But you have undertaken to preserve the American economy?" "Yes. . . ."

In the lengthy prepared statement Wallace submitted to the committee, he made it clear that he had plenty of ideas about remaking the world and that, if Congress approved his nomination, he would use the F.L.A.'s vague and extensive powers most definitely to determine the country's social character. He showed in detail how he would dish out the Federal funds to implement the "economic bill of rights" outlined in Roosevelt's January 6 message to Congress: prevention of unemployment, maintenance of wages (he even endorsed the guaranteed-annual-wage plan now being pushed by the C.I.O.), support for farm prices, financing of small business, expanding social security, Federal "plans" for housing, medical care, education. At the end, the conservative Senator George summed up the Senatorial reaction: "I think you gave us a statement that was very desirable and—I hope I don't offend you when I say—idealistic." And Senator Bailey remarked with alarm: "He [Wallace] disclosed not only a program but a method. There was nothing I could see but borrowing and lending money. I am against money spending, and I think this Government is in great danger from it. I am not going to vote to put any man in charge of a department of this Government who is going to bring in the millennium by handing out money in all directions."

Wallace's chances of retaining F.L.A. were not increased by the letter Roosevelt wrote dismissing Jones, which praised Jones's record, said nothing of any policy reasons for making the change, and was frank to the point of crudity about the political motive behind the shift: that Wallace had been useful during the campaign and was being paid off for services rendered. Roosevelt was rarely crude unless he wanted to be, and the tone of his letter seemed deliberately provocative, considering that he must have been aware of Jones's great popularity with Congress, and Wallace's equally great lack of it. His calculation may well have been to dismiss Jones in such a way that Wallace would either fail of confirmation as Secretary of Commerce or else would at least be stripped of control over F.L.A. This suspicion is strengthened by his silence all through the lengthy struggle over the appointment; not a word did he say in support of his nominee; the inflammatory letter dismissing Jones was his only public statement on the whole business. Henry, of course, "remained loyal," and when Congress confirmed his nomination after having first separated F.L.A. from Commerce and thus removed his main motive for wanting the job, he dutifully went along. Although he had stated publicly that unless F.L.A. was included he did not want the job, now he decided it was his clear duty to the common man to become Secretary of Commerce. *There is no recorded case of Henry Wallace's separating himself, on an issue of principle, either from power or from those who dispense it.*

Wallace's year and a half as Secretary of Commerce was a lull in his career, of interest mainly for two reasons: (1) His Stalinoid connections were constantly more intimate, so that the peculiar situation came about that the Secretary of Commerce was more and more a Communist fellow-traveler. The looseness of American political alignments is illustrated in this, as well as Wallace's peculiar genius for getting into false situations. (2) Stalinoid though he was, Wallace as always made little connection between his general political philosophy and his specific policies. Thus he passed over the liberal Wilson Wyatt for the undersecretaryship and appointed instead Alfred Schindler, a conservative St. Louis businessman who had served under Jones. And his choice for the top job of Director of Domestic Commerce was another conservative businessman, Albert J. Browning ("a businessman's businessman" according to *Time,* January 18, 1945), who at once began to demand incentive wages. Another embarrassment was the Small Business Advisory Committee, which Wallace set up in the Department and whose policy recommendations have been, to say the least, not very liberal.

The general Wallesian strategy in the Department of Commerce was characteristic: he ignored the only business group that had loyally fought for him during the struggle for confirmation by the Senate—the "Businessmen for Wallace"—and tried to conciliate the powerful big business forces. The result was also typical: just as all his concessions to the conservative "four-hundred-acre farmers" while he was in Agriculture have not created for him any "grass-roots" following today among farmers, so all his overtures to the business community while he was in Commerce have not won him any support among businessmen. The net result of this amateurish Machiavellian maneuvering has been just about zero. For Wallace since 1940 has been increasingly tied up with a tendency which both farmers and businessmen—not to mention the majority of organized labor—regard with implacable hostility: the "line" of the American Communist Party.

THE COMMON MAN GETS THE ATOM BOMB

In 1934, Henry Wallace wrote: "I should like to find scientists insisting that the benefactions of science be used only in ways that are plainly in the general welfare. It would be encouraging to find, among scientists everywhere, some evidence of honest indignation at the way the gifts of science have been turned against society." [42]

In 1947, Henry Wallace said: "Churchill comes out very strongly for all the glories of Western Christian civilization, and proposes to set up that civilization by the power of the atom bomb. Now, my knowledge of Christianity leads me to believe that you can't put Christianity into power by force, and if you do try to put it into a supreme position by force, the result is not Christianity but something else." [43]

May we then conclude that, at least on the question of The Bomb, Henry Wallace has consistently stuck to humanitarian principles? Alas, no. He was, on the contrary, one of the godfathers of The Bomb. Early in the war, Roosevelt created a secret policy group to study the possible use of atomic energy as a military weapon. Its members included Bush, Conant, Marshall, Stimson—and Wallace. In June, 1942, this group recommended a vast expansion of the work and the transfer of the bulk of the program to the War Department. This was the birth of the Manhattan Project.*

These three points in Wallace's thinking on the bomb may be diagrammed as follows:

1934: no bomb, no war; Henry calls on scientists to insist that their work be used only for "the general welfare."

1942: war, bomb coming up; Henry helps develop the Manhattan Project. Purpose: to defend civilization "by the power of the atom bomb."

1947: no war, bomb here, Russia on the short end; Henry discovers that civilization can no longer be defended "by the power of the atom bomb."

---

* In *The Roosevelt I Knew*, Frances Perkins writes: "He [Roosevelt] gave the signal to go ahead on the exploration and development of the atomic bomb because of his hunch that Einstein, like his fellow-scientists, was truthful and wise. He had seen him on Henry Wallace's recommendation, and he knew Wallace, a man of scientific understanding, was also truthful and wise." When I saw Wallace, I asked him about this; he said the story was untrue. Queried, Miss Perkins wrote: "I speak from memory and second-hand information. If Mr. Wallace says it is not correct, I agree."

It might be added that, far from feeling any guilt about his part in planning the atomic bomb, Henry seems to regard the whole business as a peculiar triumph of the New Deal. Writing in *The New Republic*'s commemorative issue on Roosevelt (April 15, 1946), he observed, in the course of an article entitled "He Led the Common Man":

"Roosevelt was not a scientist, but he had an intuition which made him respond to the suggestions of scientists. The outstanding example, of course, was the way he acted at once on Einstein's atomic-bomb suggestion in the fall of 1939. It took the highest sort of executive courage to pour more than two billion dollars into an utterly untried project. No President ever had such a remarkable combination of courage and imagination. Without that imaginative courage, America would not today be the world's greatest democratic nation."

4. Editor of "The New Republic" (1946—?)

ON DECEMBER 16, 1946, the first issue of the new *New Republic,* Henry Wallace, Editor, appeared, complete with a cops-and-robbers account of The Editor's Promethean agonies on behalf of the Common Man, a full-page woodcut of The Editor in the Russian ikonographic style, and an editorial by The Editor, entitled "Jobs, Peace, Freedom," which, in several thousand ill-chosen words, put him squarely on record in favor of all three.*

The first thing to be noted about Henry Wallace, Editor, is that he is not an editor.† When I interviewed him, I asked whether he passed on the articles printed in his magazine. He replied that he hoped to get time to do so later on, but that up to then he had been wholly occupied with writing editorials and answering his mail. Whatever human frailties Wallace may have, laziness is not one of them, so we may assume that it does not take him a full working-

---

* Equally bold was the keynote of The Editor's speech at an inaugural luncheon in the Waldorf-Astoria: "I lay down the challenge of battle to the Republican Party utterly and completely!"

† "EDIT—1. To oversee the preparation for publication; conduct, as a periodical."—Funk & Wagnalls Desk Dictionary.

week to answer letters and write two thousand words of rough-hewn prose. At *The New Republic* Wallace spends his time in *being* rather than *doing:* he simply exists as a Public Figure, a Spokesman around whom Support is Rallied; his workbench is the speaker's platform rather than the editorial desk, his vehicle is the daily press rather than the magazine he allegedly edits. Here, as in all departments of Wallace's present existence, it is the eidolon, Henry Wallace, that exists rather than any thinking, feeling, doing, flesh-and-blood human individual. The connection of Henry Wallace, Editor, with *The New Republic* is, in short, symbiotic rather than organic. ("SYMBIOSIS—The consorting together or partnership of dissimilar organisms.")

The idea of editorial responsibility appears to be alien to Wallace. He has shown, on occasion, a tendency to Get Out From Under when the magazine makes a bloomer. Thus, in the December 30, 1946, issue, a letter from Bernard Baruch complained that an article in a previous issue had falsely stated that his advice had been largely responsible for Truman's policy in the coal strike. Wallace replied that he "personally . . . had nothing to do with the story" and shifted the onus for the mistake onto the author of the article. The reaction of journalists to this was violent: an editor publicly takes responsibility for whatever appears in his paper. Such, at least, is the custom of the reactionary press. Wallace also complained that Baruch's letter "assumes that I personally committed an error." (Baruch had simply used the usual "Sir" of letters-to-the-editor.) Messiahs tend to confuse the personal and the impersonal, or, rather, to reduce everything to the personal. Which is one among many reasons why they are poor editors.

THE SENILITY OF YOUTH

The editorial masthead of the new *New Republic* reads like the roster of the Guatemalan army: there are an Editor (Wallace), a Publisher (Straight), an Associate Publisher, an Editorial Director, a Managing Editor, six Article Editors, eight Staff Contributors, and eleven Department Heads. The output of this imposing hierarchy is a magazine which is twice as big and half as good as the old *New Republic*. Bureaucratization is usually a disease of the old age of organizations, but this enterprise seems to have *started* its life in a state of senility. In this respect, as in the quantitative upsurge and qualitative decline, the new *New Republic* is a real child of the times. Three points about its editorial setup are worth noting:

(1) The real power behind the facade is the man who puts up the money: Michael Straight, the twenty-nine-year-old son of the late Willard Straight, a J. P. Morgan partner who gave the cash to found the magazine in 1914. Straight money has been behind *The New Republic* ever since; after the elder Straight's death, his widow, Mrs. Leonard Elmhirst of London, continued to meet the deficit. Now the younger Straight has taken over and seems to be prepared to spend large amounts of cash and enthusiasm, with both of which he is well supplied, to make it into a Big Thing. Unfortunately—judging from his published work—he knows as much about journalism as his banker father did.

(2) The old editorial staff has been purged with Soviet thoroughness. The only old editor who retains any power is Bruce Bliven, and even his post of "Editorial Director" is

said to be largely honorific. Bliven had already half purged
the other old-guard editors; when Straight returned from
the wars last spring, he eliminated Bliven after a sharp
struggle. Today such old standbys as George Soule and
Stark Young have lost even their formal status as editors.
The old Contributing Editors—including H. N. Brailsford,
E. C. Lindeman, and Rexford Tugwell—have all been
dropped.

(3) The new editors have three things in common: (a)
they are young (their average age is thirty-one); (b) they
are veterans of World War II; (c) they are former employees of the big-money press: Hearst, Luce, Conde Nast,
McCall's, The Wall Street Journal.

There are two aspects under which this enterprise may
be considered.

The first is simply as journalism. Here what strikes one
at once is that, from that Free Enterprise point of view
dear to Henry Wallace, Straight's bright young men are
not very enterprising. When Henry Luce and Harold Ross
set out to follow in the path of Horatio Alger in the
twenties, they each had an original and untried journalistic
idea, which they have slowly developed into big-circulation
magazines of the appropriate mediocrity. Even the *Readers
Digest*—also in the twenties—began as a new journalistic
idea. In each case, something was started which violated
the then established pattern in order later on to supersede
it with a new one, as in the case of the supersession of
The Literary Digest by *Time* and of *Judge* and the old
Life by *The New Yorker.* But the new *New Republic*
violates no pattern; it works with the commercial formulas long ago developed by Ross, Wallace (DeWitt), and

Luce—there is even a female research staff, who "check" all articles by putting a verifying dot over each word, just as at *Time*. Even the slight amount of originality involved in applying these formulas to liberal journalism was preempted by Ingersoll with *PM*. The average calendar age of the editors may be thirty-one, but their average journalistic age is closer to sixty. They seem unable even to transplant the slick techniques they presumably learned as bright young hucksters working for Luce or Hearst. The new *New Republic* has the defects of both the commercial and the "little" magazine, without the virtues of either: it has the banality of the former without its slick competence; it has the amateurishness of the latter without its freshness and intellectual seriousness.

THE HUCKSTERS GO LIBERAL

The other aspect under which the new *New Republic* may be considered is the qualitative. When I say it is only half as good as the old one, I do not intend any fulsome compliment to the latter. Like the rival *Nation, The New Republic* deteriorated greatly in the last decade. Their decline began with their acquiescence in the Moscow Trials of 1936-1937, the great moral watershed of the contemporary Left, and continued as World War II subjected their ideology to stresses it could not withstand. It is a melancholy exercise to compare the pre-1936 issues with later ones: the former's superiority is striking as to courage, honesty, and intellectual level.

There is, nonetheless, a significant difference in level between the old and the new *New Republics*. The latter follows *PM,* as noted above, in applying commercial techniques to the popularization of liberal ideas—or what seemed to be liberal ideas until this happened to them. Culturally, this is another instance of that merging of lowbrow and highbrow, avant-garde and commercial, which seems to be going on in all departments of American culture today. The competition between Popular Culture and High Culture is taking a new form: as in the business world, competition is now resulting in a merger. As in politics, everything and everybody are being integrated into the official culture-structure. All this is not a raising of the level of Popular Culture, as it might superficially appear to be, but rather a corruption of High Culture. There is nothing more vulgar than sophisticated *kitsch*.

Politically, this tendency is equally ruinous. To attempt to propagate political ideas on a mass scale today results in either corrupting them or draining them of all emotional force and intellectual meaning. The very media by which one must communicate with a large audience—the radio, the popular press, the movies—are infected; the language and symbols of mass communication are infected. This dismal judgment is confirmed by the experiences of *PM* and the new *New Republic*: the concessions made to demagogy and superficiality in order to attract, or even be comprehensible to, a large audience whose cultural reactions have been conditioned by life-long exposure to *kitsch*; and the necessity of using the degraded and/or simple-minded type of journalists who will put up with this sort of thing—both these factors almost guarantee corruption in advance. That neither journal so far has attracted a very large audience is another matter, due perhaps to technical defects, perhaps to the resistance of the American mass audience to liberal ideas in any form, but certainly not to any squeamishness on the editors' part.

If Henry Wallace's *New Republic* is a long step down from Bruce Bliven's, it is even farther below Herbert Croly's. When Croly founded the magazine in 1914, he defined its aim as: "Less to inform or entertain readers than to start little insurrections in the realm of their convictions." Henry Wallace's aim is not to inform or entertain, and certainly not to start mental insurrections, but simply to sell a political line with all the demagogy of the advertising profession and all the monotonous insistence on one-sided virtue of the political propagandist. As Bliven put it to a staff member, since departed: *We are going to be positive, constructive. We want journalism, not criticism.* Or as another editor said to a reviewer (also since departed): *From now on, we're going to LIKE things!* When Wallace took over, he said: "I want it to be so simple that high-school students can understand it, and so sound that doctors of philosophy respect it." The new *New Republic* has realized at least the first of those aims.

5. Henry Wallace and the U.S.S.R.

A LARGE POWER-MASS like the Soviet Union exercises a tremendous gravitational pull on an erratic comet like Henry Wallace. In the past year, this pull has become so powerful—or the resistance has been so weakened—that Wallace's Comet appears to have become a satellite of the larger body.

It was not always so. Before he became global-minded, Henry Wallace, like any other solid Iowan, used to damn "communism, fascism, and nazism" in one breath.[44] "Communism and fascism have a striking similarity," he said in 1935. "They build up a sense of national unity very much like the unity engendered by a war. Like war, they begin and end with physical force and their final outcome is likely to be as futile and devastating." [45] As late as April 9, 1941, in his Foreign Policy Association speech, he denounced "the Communists, the Nazis and the defeatists" for "weakening our efforts at economic defense." The shift in his views must, therefore, be attributed not to any personal conversion or scholarly investigation but to the simple fact that on June 25, 1941, the armies of Hitler marched against the Soviet Union, transforming Russia, in spite of herself, from the sleeping partner of fascism into a peace-loving, progressive democracy. The transformation in Henry Wallace was equally profound.

After that event, Wallace began to talk in *PM* language about "world democracy" and other ominous topics. His change of mind was strategic rather than ideological: he still praises capitalism and Free Enterprise and still deplores the class struggle, even when his specific analysis sounds like a *Pravda* editorial. The strategy was to take advantage of the political opportunity that opened up on the Left as Roosevelt's war policies turned "realistic." There were many competitors for leadership on the Right, but Roosevelt's abandonment of New Dealism left a vacuum on the Left, into which Wallace was delighted to rush. Why not a New Deal war? There was a ready-made audience for this kind of rhetoric: the Stalinoids.* Wallace began to talk to them, and they in turn influenced him. Their ruthless energy appealed to his pragmatic side; they knew what they wanted and how to get it—qualities that were both impressive and useful to a man of Wallace's temperament; their enthusiasm for fine phrases matched his own. It was a marriage of convenience that developed into a love match.

By 1941, there was also a personal influence at work on him.

ENTER HAROLD YOUNG

During the 1940 campaign, Wallace became associated with two individuals who were, to say the least, not the type his admirers would have expected to be his close

---

* This term is used to indicate a general adherence to the Communist Party line of the moment. It embraces party members, fellow-travelers, and the vast army of "innocent" dupes. Others listened to Wallace with sympathy, of course, but the Stalinoids provided both the brain trust and the cadres.

advisers. One was Charles Marsh, a wealthy Texas oil man and chain-newspaper publisher, who was introduced to Wallace by Roosevelt. Just why Marsh was a Roosevelt man is not clear. His papers were straight commercial enterprises, his associates were the "Texas Regulars"—the Jesse Jones crowd that tried to ditch Roosevelt in 1944— and his general behavior seems to have been about what one would expect of a rich Texan; perhaps it was an old man's whim; perhaps other considerations played a part. At any rate, Marsh is said to have financed Wallace's 1940 vice-presidential campaign. He also introduced into Wallace's entourage, as campaign-manager, his handyman and protégé, another Texan: a lawyer-lobbyist named Harold Young. For the next six years, Young was to be Wallace's *alter ego* and most trusted political adviser. He served as "special assistant" during Wallace's vice-presidential term; ran the campaign to get the 1944 renomination at Chicago; and occupied the important post of Solicitor-General of the Department of Commerce during Wallace's term as Secretary. Although Young did not accompany Wallace to *The New Republic,* he still works closely with him and is currently running a "Wallace headquarters" in Washington.

A more vivid personal contrast to Wallace could hardly be found: Young is a big, fat, high-living, back-slapping character, loud of mouth and brash of manner, with a perpetual cigar stuck in the corner of his mouth—in short, the classic type of American ward politician. "Practical politics" is his specialty, although there is some doubt, despite his authentic vulgarity, as to just how smart he really is. His ego is as little in need of expansion as his waist-line: he apparently treated Wallace with the paternalistic insolence of a worldly-wise big brother toward the shy "intellectual" of the family. Comic situations resulted when earnest delegations for some worthy cause were shunted off to see Wallace's personal representative and found themselves confronting a replica of Big Bill Thompson. Or when, substituting for Henry at liberal dinners, this tough Texas politico sounded off about racial democracy.

One may guess that Wallace, not an acute judge of people, was impressed by Young's down-to-earth manner. One may also guess that he was not at all bothered by the contrast between Young's "practical politics" and his own lofty moralizing, for Wallace has always kept his ideals uncontaminated by contact with his political actions. For him, the real and the ideal exist on different planes, neither inhibiting the free expansion of the other.

Whatever the rationale of the Young-Wallace relationship, those who ought to know insist that the Stalinoid alliance was largely Young's idea, and that it was through Young that fellow-travelers like Harry Bridges had access to Wallace. There was no question of any ideological sympathy, of course. It probably seemed to Young "smart politics" to play in with the Stalinoids, as in fact it was during the war; it would have been even smarter, however, to have advised Henry to let go of the bear's tail after 1945, something which Young seems to have neglected to do.

. . . AND DAVID KARR

During this period, Wallace acquired another close associate whose personality would have disturbed his libera public: an energetic young-man-on-the-make named David Karr, a real-life version of the Hollywood "hot shot" reporter. Even his fellow newsmen, no violets themselves, are awed by Karr's colossal nerve. They tell how he used to hang around the Washington airport till he spotted a celebrity getting off a plane, whereupon he would rush up, warmly shake hands, grab the celebrity's bag, and offer him a lift into town; how he breezed into cabinet members' offices, uninvited and sometimes unannounced, slapped his notebook down, and commanded: "Give!"; how he introduced Willkie to Molotov at a Washington reception without benefit of a previous acquaintance with either. His colleagues also regard him, respectfully though not admiringly, as "smart" and skilled in fighting. Such was the man who ghosted many of Wallace's inspirational war-aims speeches and became a permanent fixture in the Vice-President's office.

During the war, Karr went from the O.F.F. to a forty-six-thousand-dollar executive job in O.W.I. He is now a "leg man" for Drew Pearson at a salary estimated at between fifteen and twenty thousand dollars a year. At least one Common Man seems to have found his Century.

There is another aspect of Wallace's wartime ghostwriter which is perhaps worth passing notice. In the House, on February 18, 1944, Representative Busbey of Illinois stated: "Mr. Speaker, I have been informed that Vice-President Wallace has recently returned to Washington after one of his extended journeys. . . . Accompanying him, as a member of his entourage, was one David Karr. Mr. Karr, by his own testimony under oath before the Committee on Un-American Activities on April 6, 1943, admitted having been a writer for *The Daily Worker,* and also for *Equality,* a Communist-front publication, as well as having lectured for the American League for Peace and Democracy. . . . Mr. Speaker, some of us are wondering if when we hear the voice of Henry Agard Wallace, we are listening to the words of David Karr." It is only fair to add that (a) Karr today vehemently denies any sympathy for the Commies, and (b) diligent inquiry has revealed nothing concrete to disprove his assertion. It *would* be interesting to know, however, whether he ghosted Wallace's speech at the Soviet Friendship Rally on November 8, 1942.

THE "FREE WORLD" SPEECH

Not the least of Wallace's debt to the Stalinoids is the job they did on the speech which established him in his present role of prophet of "global" democracy: the 1942 "Free World" speech. The story of how it chanced to become the Gettysburg Address of the liberals is worth telling.

With one exception, the newspapers reported Wallace's speech in perfunctory fashion; the "angle" they chose was a minor point about the defense of Alaska; not even *The New York Times* bothered to print the complete text; the shimmering ideological exhalations were left to expire, unreported, in the New Worlders' banqueting hall. The exception was the Stalinoid daily, *PM.* And even *PM's* secondary editors had prepared a routine treatment of the speech, also stressing the Alaska defense angle and omitting the "common man" rhapsodies. But Ralph McAllister Ingersoll, editor-in-chief, chanced to have heard the speech delivered; he rang up his staff at three A.M. and asked how they were going to handle it. They told him. Ingersoll exploded, ordered the whole make-up "torn up," the complete text of the speech printed, and the front page devoted to "plugging" it as a great expression of war aims. The editor in charge of the issue disagreed violently, insisting that the speech was cheap demagogy with totalitarian overtones. He refused to "build it up" as Ingersoll required and staged a one-man sit-down strike in a near-by bar. Ingersoll finally had to taxi out to Brooklyn and do the dirty work himself.

PM came out hours late the next day, but it was worth it. Ingersoll's flair for liberal journalism had not betrayed him: *PM* made the speech famous, and the speech won great prestige for *PM* among liberals hungry for rationalizations about the war. With typical Stalinoid cynicism, Ingersoll worked up a noisy campaign about the "deliberate suppression" of Wallace's speech by the capitalist press (although his own editors had also been about to "suppress" it). Telegrams were dispatched to leading journalists asking them what they thought about this heinous plot against the common man; the replies were, of course, satisfactorily indignant and made more front-page copy for *PM*. The ballyhoo reached such proportions that other papers felt obliged, days later, to take extended notice of the speech. Nor should we omit the contribution of another high personage: A. N. Spanel, president of the International Latex Corporation, who heard the speech on the radio and at once bought space in *The Washington Post* to reprint it as a full-page ad.

It is distressing to have to report that later on Wallace behaved with characteristic ingratitude. He was always willing to listen to Ingersoll's advice as to how to propagandize the Common Man theme. But when it came to giving someone an inside track on news in the B.E.W., Wallace tended to favor powerful conservative papers instead of the maverick *PM*. After this had happened several times, Ingersoll blew up: *That goddamned doublecrossing soandso! Christ! We MADE the guy!*

RUSSIA: THE GENERAL LINE

Other instances of Wallace's Stalinoid connections could be given. In recent New York City elections, for example, he campaigned for three Congressional candidates who are notoriously close to the comrades: A. Clayton Powell, Jr.; Johannes Steel; and Vito Marcantonio. Of the last, the only man in Congress who consistently follows the Communist Party line, Wallace stated on November 5, 1946: "Marcantonio has the best voting record of all the 435 members of Congress." (That Steel and Marcantonio were both running against regular Democratic candidates did not bother Wallace, although a few months earlier he had demanded the expulsion from the party of Democratic congressmen who did not follow the party line.) Last October, Wallace was accompanied on his speaking tour of the West Coast by ex-Representative Hugh De Lacy of Washington, who in 1940 cast the only vote in the Democratic Convention against Roosevelt's renomination (that was the "Yanks Are Not Coming" period), and who was recently described by *The Nation* as "a man whose fundamental loyalty seems to be to the Communist Party line." [46]

Wallace's relations with Steel—another overripe character, by the way; Henry has a genius for getting mixed up with them—appear to be most friendly. "To my mind," he wrote Steel on February 7, 1946, "you have carried on the fight against worldwide fascism with great courage and determination . . . on behalf of the common man." (That man is here again.) Steel preceded Wallace to Europe this spring, armed with letters of introduction, as a kind of advance scout. He covered the Moscow Conference for a small-circulation "newsletter" he edits. He was not among the thirty-five reporters chosen by the United States press to fill the strict quota allowed by the Russians; but the Soviet Government, for some reason or other, gave him a visa anyway.

Such personal links—not counterbalanced, so far as I can discover, by association with people critical of Soviet policy—show that Wallace is not, as he affects to be, a sincere liberal trying to be "fair" to Russia, but rather an apologist for Stalinism. But even more conclusive evidence is to be found in his public utterances since 1941.

Wallace's "general line" on Russia was memorably expressed in his speech at the Soviet Friendship Rally in Madison Square Garden on November 8, 1942. Excerpts:

"Some in the United States believe that we have over-emphasized what might be called political or Bill-of-Rights democracy. . . . Its extreme form leads to exploitation. Russia, perceiving some of the abuses of excessive political democracy, has placed strong emphasis on economic democracy. . . . Carried to an extreme, all power is centered in one man. . . . Somewhere there is a practical balance between economic and political democracy. . . . The chief difference between the economic organization of Russia and that of the United States is that it is almost impossible to live on income-producing property in Russia. . . . In present-day Russia, differences in wage income are almost but not quite as great as in the United States."

Only Wallace could compress so much falsification, confusion, and evasion into so short a space. There is no "economic democracy" in Russia, unless the absence of private ownership be considered *ipso facto* democratic: workers are tied to their jobs; they have no say about wages or working conditions; their unions are company unions. Far from being a way of correcting the abuses of what Wallace calls "excessive political democracy," the Russian economic system is a slave system precisely because there is no political democracy (and who but Wallace would split democracy in half and expect the two halves to live?). Income differences in Russia are considerably *greater* than in this country. The chief difference between the two systems, from the worker's standpoint, is that in the U.S.A. he has *some* freedom of movement and *some* power to protect his interests, while in the U.S.S.R. he has none. Has Russian "economic democracy" been carried to the extreme where "all power is centered in one man" or has it not? Wallace neglects to say. He is also disingenuous when he pretends to be holding the scales evenly between the two systems. His speech lists five kinds of democracy: political, economic, ethnic, educational, and sexual. Rigged this way, the contest adds up in Wallace's box score: U.S.S.R. 3, U.S.A. 1, with one game (sexual) tied.

In the spring of 1944, Roosevelt sent Wallace on a "goodwill" mission to China and Soviet Asia. (Wallace is the ideal envoy for such empty pilgrimages.) Never has one man learned so little from so much travel. In *Soviet Asia Mission* (1946), Wallace describes his trip. He begins by thanking eight individuals for their assistance in preparing the book. Four names I don't recognize; the four I do are all Stalinoids of long standing. Before he left the United States Wallace knew just what he would find in Soviet Asia:

"It is with great anticipation that I approach the Siberian experience. . . . Over 40,000,000 people have taken the place of the 7,000,000—mostly convicts—who miserably existed there under Imperial Russia. So the detractors of Russia must pause before the fact of Soviet Asia of today. . . . I shall see the cities. I shall feel the grandeur that comes when men work wisely with nature."

The rest of the book lives up to the opening. There are rhapsodies about collective farming which almost convince one that Wallace doesn't know anything even about agriculture. Compulsion everywhere appears to him as the spontaneous will of the people. At Krasnoyarsk he notes: "The war-bond drive has been well-organized, for he [the Soviet officer in charge] said that purchases by the employees averaged 12 per cent of their earnings. 'Often,' he added, 'patriotic individuals turn in all their savings.'" Apparently unaware that the N.K.V.D. is the chief recruiter of labor-power for Soviet Asia, he approvingly quotes another local chieftain: "'I could use a million people right now in the Amur region.'" At Irkutsk he makes a speech comparing modern Siberia with the nineteenth-century American frontier and declaring that "men born in wide free spaces will not brook injustice" and "will not even temporarily live in slavery." As noted above, Wallace thinks that under the Czar the inhabitants of Siberia were "mostly convicts," whereas today they are free-hearted Soviet pioneers. The actuality is the reverse: the Czarist deportations were on a minuscule scale compared to the long trains of cattle-cars crammed with millions of "kulaks" and "antisocial elements" (including grandmothers and babes in arms) that have poured labor-power, in the form of political exiles, year after year into Stalin's Siberia.* "I can bear witness," continued Wallace to the assembled and stupefied prison-camp wardens of Irkutsk, "I can bear witness to the willingness with which your citizens give their utmost efforts in mines, aircraft factories, and metallurgical works."

There are two references to Trotsky in the book. (1) " 'This kind of thing,' he [a local official] said, referring to the new towns we had seen, 'this kind of thing, Trotsky was against.' " (2) "I was interested to hear that on this issue [collectivization of agriculture] Stalin and Trotsky were in fundamental disagreement. Dimitri Chavakhim of the Soviet Foreign Affairs Office explained it this way: 'Trotsky wanted to make peace with the kulaks. . . .' " The most superficial acquaintance with the 1920–1930 period of

* Cf. *Russia in Perspective* (1947), by George Soloveytchik, which cites the definitive study of Czarist deportations, George Kennan's *Siberia and the Exile System* (1891). Kennan's two main findings: (1) in the sixty-four year period, 1823–1887, the total number of exiles deported to Siberia was 772,979; (2) of these the great majority were nonpolitical criminals and their families (who went *voluntarily*, not, as under Stalin, compulsorily), the total number of "politicals banished by administrative process" being for the representative period 1879–1884, exactly 749! If we take the lowest estimate that has been made of the number of persons sent into exile by the Stalin regime—ten million—we find that in twenty years Stalin has exiled thirteen times as many persons as the Czars did in sixty-four years. And, furthermore, that practically all of Stalin's exiles were *political* deportees, as against less than 1 per cent of the Czars' exiles.

Russian history would have told Wallace that (1) rapid industrialization was the key point of the program of Trotsky's opposition, with Stalin consistently opposed to it; and (2) it was Trotsky who pressed for collectivization of agriculture, while Stalin took the side of the kulaks and N.E.P.-men in holding it back. After exiling Trotsky in 1928, Stalin adopted his program almost *in toto,* retroactively revising the whole history of his conflict with Trotsky. It is evidently this revision which Wallace—or, rather, his Stalinoid ghost writers—prefers to accept. To insist on this point is sheer pedantry, since Trotsky is dead, Stalin is in power, and Henry Wallace is no more ignorant than a dozen other eminent American innocents abroad.

During his term as Secretary of Commerce, Wallace became more and more openly a spokesman for Russian policy inside the cabinet. Thus, on September 21, 1945, he proposed at a cabinet meeting that Britain and the United States reveal the secret of the atomic bomb to Russia as "peace insurance." His argumentation was naive even for Henry: "Those who share the Secretary's view," states one account, "contend that as a result of turning the secret over to Russia, that nation would be placed under a perpetual moral obligation never to use the atomic bomb against any of the Allied conquerors of the Axis power." Throughout the period from the Potsdam Agreement (August, 1945) to Secretary Byrnes's Stuttgart speech (September, 1946) when Soviet diplomacy was on the offensive and the Western powers were following an appeasement policy, Wallace uttered no public criticism of Russia's ever increasing demands. On the contrary, he apologized for them in formulations—doubtless supplied by his Stalinoid advisers and ghost writers—which closely followed the Kremlin's line of the moment. A typical instance was the debate with W. Averell Harriman at a dinner of the American Society for Russian Relief. Harriman, who had just retired as United States Ambassador in Moscow, criticized Russia's foreign policy as unilateral, aggressive, and destructive of world peace. "Mr. Wallace expounded the view that Russia was taking what it conceived to be 'its only road to peace and security,' not war. He spoke of its fears and desires, fears of 'capitalist encirclement,' the desire to make 'every boundary secure'; 'the fear of little time in which to make ready for a possible capitalist-provoked war.' " [47] This is a good example of the double standard in political morality which Wallace has consistently applied to Russia: her imperialistic behavior is to be understood—and, by implication, forgiven —because it has certain historical causes; but when Britain or the United States acts imperialistically, the question of causation is dropped and the issue becomes simply a moral one. The general idea is that the Western powers must have a higher standard of international ethics than Russia. Or, as he put it a year later in a speech in England: "You will tell me that Russia is expansionist. . . . I do not deny it, but I say that it is the task of the countries which have the atomic bomb and which have not, like Russia, been devastated by war and boycotted in peace, to use power to create world prosperity and increase abundance." [48] All these arguments could have been applied to Hitler's Germany between 1934 and 1939: her economic position was desperate, her fears of "encirclement" and her desire to "make every boundary secure" were as strong as those of Russia today, she was "boycotted in peace" from the Versailles Treaty on, etc. The moral duty of the richer Western powers to "create world prosperity" by a policy of sympathy and understanding was thus equally imperative. Such arguments were in fact raised, and such a policy was in fact carried out. Its architects were Chamberlain and Daladier, its name was "appeasement," and its end result was Munich.

When Byrnes, at Stuttgart, dropped appeasement of Russia, Wallace's reaction was so violent as to carry him out of the cabinet altogether.

THE MADISON SQUARE GARDEN SPEECH

On September 12, 1946, Wallace spoke to a Stalinoid audience in New York City's Madison Square Garden. After a preliminary plea for "peace"—in which he characteristically noted: "I say this as one who steadfastly backed preparedness throughout the thirties. We have no use for namby-pamby pacifism."—he developed the main body of his argument:

"We may not like what Russia does in Eastern Europe. Her type of land reform, industrial expropriation and suppression of basic liberties offends the great majority of the people of the United States. On our part, we should recognize that we have no more business in the political affairs of Eastern Europe than Russia has in the political affairs of Latin America, Western Europe and the United States. But whether we like it or not, the Russians will try to socialize their sphere of influence, just as we try to democratize our sphere of influence. . . .

"Russian ideals of social-economic justice are going to govern nearly a third of the world. Our ideas of free-enterprise democracy will govern much of the rest. . . . By mutual agreement, this competition should be put on a friendly basis, and the Russians should stop conniving against us in certain areas just as we should stop scheming against them in other parts of the world. . . .

"Once the fears of Russia and the United States have been allayed by practical regional political reservations, I am sure that concern over the veto power will be greatly diminished. Then the United Nations would have a really great power in those areas which are truly international and not regional. In the world-wide, as distinguished from the regional field, the armed might of the United Nations should be so great as to make opposition useless. . . . In brief, as I see it, today the world order is bankrupt, and the United States, Russia and England are the receivers. These are the hard facts of power politics on which we have to build a functioning, powerful United Nations and a body of international law. As we build, we must develop fully the doctrine of the rights of small nations."

Wallese has seldom reached greater heights. An ideal world is to be built on power politics; the United Nations are to rule everywhere except where the big powers don't want them to; the "world order" is bankrupt and the Big Three are the only real forces today; therefore they "must" protect the rights of small nations—except in "regional" areas, that is in the one-third of the world which "Russian ideas . . . are going to govern" and "much of the rest" which *our* ideas will rule. This leaves Patagonia and possibly the headwaters of the Niger as the field of action of the United Nations.

The political heart of the speech is the delicate term, "practical regional political reservations," by which is meant simply spheres of influence. The former One Worlder proposes now Two Worlds, since this is more to Russia's advantage at the present moment. Wallace's proposal is analagous to those of the old pro-Nazi isolationists: let Hitler (Stalin) run his sphere, while we run ours; of course, the Nazi (Soviet) "ideals of socio-economic justice" are not ours, but there is room in the world for both, etc., etc. This attitude is immoral because it accepts evil—the Nazi (or Soviet) horrors—as a status quo to be let alone, for expediency's sake, by people whose own ethical concepts are alleged to be different and better. It is also as clearly opposed to the national interest of American imperialism as was the pro-Nazi line. In this sense, Wallace is an American fifth-columnist. It is hypocrisy for him to present his program as one of friendly cooperation between the U.S.A. and the U.S.S.R., when it is actually unilateral, giving the U.S.A. nothing it hasn't got already and giving the U.S.S.R. all it wants at present (and hasn't yet got): a free hand in the vast new sphere of influence she has acquired since the end of the war. This is simply appeasement à la Munich and would not cause Stalin to behave any more "co-operatively" than it did Hitler—or than Roosevelt's enormous and foolish concessions at Teheran and Yalta did.

Wallace's "regional" proposal shocked his Latin American admirers.* Their outcries at this "betrayal" by the

* These are, or were, numerous. Perhaps no American political leader has been so popular as Wallace in Latin America. His two Goodwill tours were great successes: he was not only obviously full of Goodwill but he had even taken the trouble to learn Spanish. The intelligentsia were especially charmed, but it is hard for the intellectuals of semicolonial lands to be critical about an American or Englishman who flatters and conciliates them.

apostle of Good Neighborliness reached such volume that Wallace went on the air a week later and tried to take it all back, "reaffirming" his One World creed and adding, "I wish to emphasize that any regionalism . . . must take into account the rights of small nations."

The comedy of errors that followed this speech was something special even in Wallace's career. (As Falstaff was said to be not only witty himself but also a cause of wit in others, so Wallace is not only confused but a cause of confusion elsewhere.) The Stalinoid audience in Madison Square Garden, disturbed by the mild criticisms Wallace felt it strategic to make of Russian policy, actually gave the speech a hostile reception, and next morning's *Daily Worker* was highly critical. It was only days later, after shrewder heads overseas had set the American comrades right, that the Party press decided the speech was not a Reactionary Mishmash but, on the contrary, a Great Progressive Document.

But this was as nothing compared to what went on in the White House. Wallace's speech was a direct criticism of Byrnes's Stuttgart address, a criticism, that is, by a leading member of the Administration of the Administration's official foreign policy. Yet when Wallace brought Truman an advance copy of the speech to read, the President found nothing to object to in it and told him to go ahead. He even said, as Wallace took care to insert into the text, that the speech "represented the policy of his Administration." When newspapermen asked him about this a few hours before the speech was to be delivered, Truman confirmed the statement. "Did it not represent a departure from Secretary

Byrnes's policy?" another reporter asked. "No," said Mr. Truman, "it was right in line." [49] The next day's dispatches from Paris made it clear, however, that Byrnes did not share the President's cheerful opinion of the speech but was, indeed, very much "bewildered" and "disturbed" about it. By the following day, September 14, even Harry Truman began to sense that life had suddenly become rather complicated. Chipper and jaunty as ever, he called in the press and told what, coming from a man in a less exalted position, would be called a lie: he had been misunderstood by the press; he had not intended to say that he approved the content of the speech but merely Wallace's right to give it. On September 18, Wallace saw Truman; on coming out, he told the press that it had been agreed that he should remain in the cabinet and that he would "make no public speeches or statements" on foreign policy until the conclusion of the Paris Conference. (*There is no recorded case of Henry Wallace's separating himself, on an issue of principle, either from power or from those who dispense it.*) On September 19, Byrnes delivered to Truman, by transatlantic teletype, an ultimatum: either Wallace or he would have to leave the cabinet. The following morning, Truman called for Wallace's resignation. The momentous news was delivered to the press by Wallace's bumptious Under-Secretary, Harold Young, with just the right low-comedy touch: emerging from Wallace's office with the valedictory statement of the Friend of the Common Man fluttering in his hand, he paused an instant, struck an attitude, and announced: *Boys, you're looking at the acting Secretary of Commerce!*

THE EUROPEAN TOUR

When Kingsley Martin, editor of the British liberal-Stalinoid weekly *The New Statesman and Nation,* invited Henry Wallace to come to England in the spring of 1947 and make a few speeches, neither he nor Wallace nor, so far as can be determined, any one else anticipated the uproar that would result. The crowds that turned out to hear Wallace in England were enormous; their enthusiasm was unbounded. At home, the American press gave him more front-page headlines than he had ever before received; the reaction to his speeches here, however, was intense rather than enthusiastic.

The reason for the warmth of the British response and the chilliness of the American was the same: Henry, as usual, was out to please his audience.

In his Madison Square Garden speech, he had pictured Britain as the seducer of an innocent United States into the ways of power politics: "To make Britain the key to our foreign policy would be, in my opinion, the height of folly. We must not let reactionary leadership force us into that position. We must not let British balance-of-power manipulations determine whether and when the United States gets into war. Make no mistake about it—the British imperialistic policy in the Near East alone . . . would lead the United States straight to war."

Now, six months later, speaking to a British audience, he reversed his field, retracting his charges of imperialism against Britain and adding: "The people of Britain have the greatest opportunity for offering true leadership to the world. . . . Britain fought in the magnificent spirit of

blood, toil, sweat and tears, and so was morally prepared
for postwar problems. . . . Your destiny is to save the
world. . . . If you show the way, all progressive peoples
can speak out for world progress." [50] As for his own country, it now became the chief obstacle to peace and progress:
"At the end of the war, America's main objective was a
quick victory, followed by a quick return to normalcy. It
was the normalcy of selfishness, nationalism and power politics." [51] Not only did he implore the British Government
not to support his own Government in its conflict with
Russia, not only did he denounce the Truman Doctrine as
imperialism (which it is) and praise British foreign policy
as peace-loving and democratic (which it isn't), but he also
presented the unique spectacle of an American politician
telling British audiences that their whole way of life was
superior to that of his own country. Not since Henry James
has an American become (temporarily, of course) such an
Anglophile.

The reaction at home was immediate and violent. For
several days, Congress spent much of its time denouncing
Wallace. Senators accused him of treason and demanded
his prosecution under the long-forgotten Logan Act, which
forbids a private citizen to deal with a foreign government
to defeat his own government's policy. These demands for
the suppression of a citizen's right to free criticism of governmental policies fortunately did not come to more than
talk—though they are ominous indications of a tendency.
But the uproar did have a practical effect, and just the opposite of what Wallace intended by his speeches: the critics
of the Truman Doctrine, fearing identification with
Henry's wild talk, retreated, and even Senator Pepper an-

nounced that he would vote for the Greek-Turkish aid bill. In fact, it is probable that much of the uproar in Congress and the press was deliberately whipped up by the Truman Administration in order to intimidate all critics of the Truman Doctrine. The headlines thus may have been less a tribute to Wallace's oratory than to the shrewdness of his opponents.

As for Russia, Wallace lost on his European tour whatever inhibitions he may have had at home. Even the delicate question of civil liberties under Stalin did not bother him. "I have a hunch," he told a British audience, "I have a hunch that if I could speak Russian, Mr. Stalin would let me speak to the common people there just as I am speaking to you." [52] Which was probably true enough, though not for the reasons implied. In Norway, he denounced the American capitalist press for suppressing and distorting the news but forgot to criticize the Russian press for the same offenses, which was like saying the trouble with Chicago under Capone was that the churches raised money by Bingo games. He also gave Stalin's dictatorship his full support against any kind of opposition from within: "It would be unfortunate for world peace if anything happens inside Russia to upset its system of government at the present time." [53]

By the time Wallace got to Paris, on April 22, he had apparently begun to worry about the reactions at home. (After all, the voters of Kansas, and not Manchester, Oslo, or Paris, will send or not send him sometime to the White House.) This anxiety was increased by the way the Communists monopolized him during his brief stay in France. His only formal welcome came from the Communist Party

—which, through its parliamentary affiliate, the Pierre Cot group, had arranged his French tour. When he spoke at the Sorbonne, the only important party leaders on the platform with him were the Communist Party trio—Thorez, Duclos, and Cachin—and the audience was almost wholly Communist. When he addressed the National Union of Intellectuals, the chairman was Louis Aragon, who later wrote, in the Stalinist daily *Ce Soir,* that Wallace reminded him strongly of Abraham Lincoln and Walt Whitman.

"I want to try to avoid being monopolized by the extreme Left, who have been so friendly to me in Paris," Wallace confided to a luncheon of the Anglo-American Press Association, adding that the differences between his viewpoint and Truman's were "not very great."

His most heroic effort at disengagement was his speech to the Paris chapter of the American Veterans Committee. Presenting himself as a good American who believes in democracy, free speech, an economy of abundance, and all other pleasant things, he criticized communism and endorsed capitalism. He explained that, when he had attacked American "ruthless imperialism" in England, he had referred not to the Government's policy but to that of James Burnham and Henry Luce. As usual, the reporters had misquoted him. He even spoke up for "the enforcement of human rights in all countries" and specifically for the work of the United Nations Human Rights Commission—though, when Mrs. Roosevelt had been struggling with the Russians in the Commission on this issue, a great silence had settled over Henry. He concluded with fulsome praise for "the splendid idealism" of Americans, including his A.V.C. audience, "in serving the peace and welfare of the world."

6. Corn-Fed Mystic

A FRIENDLY OBSERVER describes a scene in 1933 when a business delegation called on Wallace to discuss A.A.A.: "Wallace listened with about as much animation as a hitching post. . . . A fat and rather disagreeable member said that God himself couldn't make A.A.A. work. Instantly, Wallace was standing straight with raised head. He spoke easily, his eyes flashed. 'I have faith that Divine Providence will provide a means to fit the times!' " [54] One suspects that not the least of these means was to be Henry Wallace. Just as he thinks of America as the nation destined by God to lead the world, so Wallace thinks of himself as a Messiah, an instrument through whom God will guide America onward and upward.

FRUSTRATED MESSIAH

This feeling comes out strongly in *Statesmanship and Religion* (1934), a curious work in which the Old Testament prophets are pictured as New Dealers struggling against "the standpatters worshipping Baal." Especially when he denies it: "I trust we shall never have to have a prophet like Elisha, who stirred up Jehu to bloody revolution. . . . It is interesting to note that Jehu formed a compact with the Rechabites, the communists of that day. . . . Yes, I trust we shall not need Elishas and Jehus and Rechabites to cure the evils of this civilization by causing blood to flow in the streets." Wallace is a kindly man, yet I think we may detect a note of satisfaction in the idea of curing social evils by bloodshed if the stiff-necked sons of Baal refuse to listen to reason; and, if an Elisha is needed, Wallace seems not reluctant to play the role (he has already made the compact with the Rechabites). When farmers would not listen to his program in the twenties, he told a friend: "I guess we haven't suffered enough yet." [55] The theme is repeated in *Statesmanship and Religion*: "Perhaps the times will have to be even more difficult before the hearts of our people will have been moved sufficiently so they will be willing to join together in a modern adaptation of the theocracy of old." This theocracy is to be based on "a revival of deep religious feeling" that will "grow side by side with a new social discipline." A less attractive form of society could hardly be imagined.

Yet there seems in Wallace a suspicion—happily justified —that he lacks something that the Old Testament prophets had. "Of course, the outstanding characteristic of the prophets which is lacking today," he observes, "is that intensity of conviction which enabled them to say: 'Thus saith the Lord!'" [56] He adds that only three men in the twentieth century have had this "tremendous earnestness": Lenin, Hitler, and Mussolini. We may be grateful that Wallace is not a Lenin, or even a Mussolini. He would like to be: he is willing to be ruthless; he has an enormous drive for personal power; he is constantly fumbling around for a total political doctrine. But his personality is not integrated enough to enable him to stick to a few basic ideas and reject others; he is, fortunately, a dilettante, fearful of get-

ting in too deep, and an opportunist who would be all
things to all men. He has never been able to carry out his
own prescription: "The problem of statesmanship is to
mold a policy leading toward a higher state for humanity
and to stick by that policy and make it seem desirable in
spite of short-term political pressure to the contrary." [57]
One suspects that the very violence and frequency of Wallace's statements of high principle are primarily attempts
to assure himself that he *does* have convictions.

FROM CALVINISM TO THE OCCULT

Wallace was raised in the strictest of Calvinist churches:
the United Presbyterian. When he grew up, he tells us, he
was repelled by the dogmatism of the creed and the dry
intellectualism of the sermons. Dropping into a high Episcopalian service, he found that the ritual moved him deeply.
So, in 1931, he became a high Episcopalian, a characteristic
compromise between Calvinism and Roman Catholicism.
He led Bible classes, became an acolyte. "For months,
wearing a cassock and surplice, he knelt at the altar on
Sunday and regularly served 8 o'clock mass." [58]

Formal religion, however, is not the important part of
Wallace's abundant other-worldly life. He delights especially in esoteric knowledge, strange creeds in which the
scientific and the supernatural are blended. "His faith . . .
seems to be an amalgam of Buddhism, Judaism, Zoroas-
trianism, Mohammedanism, and Eddyism." [59] To which
might be added: theosophy, spiritualism, numerology, and
astrology. "Wallace dabbles in astrology and can draw a
horoscope. He is quite familiar with the theory that the
future can be predicted from certain markings on the Great

Pyramid." [60] There is some confusion, as always in trying
to define Wallace's beliefs, as to whether his interest in this
mystic lore is that of the speculative scientist or the con-
vert. Most writers, though not all, believe it to be the latter;
I agree with the majority. Paul Appleby, who served as
Wallace's personal assistant in the early years in Agriculture,
once remarked: *I don't dare let a theosophist in to see Henry
—he'd give him a job right away. I have to be careful, or
the place would be overrun with them.* Milo Perkins was
running a theosophist church in Houston, Texas, when he
first met Wallace.

Wallace's leanings toward esoteric doctrines have not
helped him politically, for there is a widespread feeling in
this country—one which I do not share—that such doctrines
are absurd in themselves. It must be admitted, however,
that Wallace's use of them—like his expositions of more
secular doctrines—has generally been foolish.

THE ROERICH STORY

After the 1934 drought, Wallace sent an expedition to
the Orient to look for certain drought-resistant grasses
which were believed to grow in Outer Mongolia and Tibet.
The expedition was composed of plant experts from the
Department of Agriculture. To head it, Wallace appointed,
without consulting anyone, a strange and quite undepart-
mental character named Nicholas Roerich, promoter of a
vague enterprise called The Roerich Pact for the Protection
of Cultural Treasures and the Promotion of World Peace.
Roerich, a white Russian, was also a painter of mystical
pictures. The talk around the Department was that someone

had persuaded the Secretary that somewhere on those remote mysterious plains would be found evidence of the Second Coming of Christ, and that Wallace had decided to combine business with pleasure. Friction developed between Roerich and the prosaic plant experts under his command. Roerich cabled Wallace demanding he recall the chief expert. Knowles Ryerson, chief of the Bureau of Plant Industry and one of the country's outstanding plant biologists, backed up his subordinate in the field. Wallace thereupon recalled the subordinate and fired Ryerson. The expedition was finally terminated hastily by the State Department after the Soviet Government had protested against political speeches Roerich had been making while traveling around Mongolia as an official United States representative. The whole affair was a dismal fiasco, discovering nothing much about either native grasses or the Second Coming. Some time later, after more experience with Roerich, Wallace acknowledged he had been in the wrong and apologized to Ryerson, who had left the Department to make a successful academic career.

THE "ZENDA" LETTERS

The most spectacular result of Wallace's esoteric propensities was the affair of the "Zenda" letters. Let it be said at once that the letters—the damaging ones at least—were *probably* forgeries. The story is worth telling, however, because (1) it is a bit of political history that has been widely talked about but has never been fully told in print; and (2) even the Democrats had to admit that the letters did not clash with the spirit of much that Wallace had indubitably written—*se non è vero, è bene trovato.*

The most extensive printed reference to the affair * occurs on page 197 of Charles Michelson's *The Ghost Talks* (1944): "During the 1940 campaign, Harry Hopkins came over to New York highly excited over a big batch of letters of at least doubtful authenticity, supposed to be from Henry Wallace. Their general purport was silly rather than evil. Hopkins assured us they were forgeries. Doubtless some of them, perhaps all, were fabrications. The Republicans had bought them, we were advised, but were afraid to put them out and could find no publisher daring enough to take the responsibility. . . . Hopkins suggested expedients that would have made admirable chapters in an Oppenheim novel (for he regarded the matter as of tragic importance) but fitted into no conception of practical politics. . . . The opposition could not find a publisher, the Democratic national organization gave them no opening, and so the storm passed without hysteria at headquarters and never figured in the campaign."

Michelson's last statement is hardly true; there was enough "hysteria" to cause him to move the entire Democratic publicity staff into New York to be ready to counterattack if the Republicans used the letters. That the letters were "silly" is also considerable of an understatement. They purported to be written by Wallace to "Zenda," a female astrologer connected with the Roerich Museum (again the Roerich thread!), who had once been on good terms with him but had since quarreled. About half were written on

* Except for Westbrook Pegler's recent columns. These are, unhappily, of little value because Pegler detests Wallace so virulently as to be unable to write coherently about him. Pegler's material is long on invective but short on concrete data.

Department stationery and were signed with Wallace's full name. Handwriting experts found these signatures to be genuine; these letters, however, were perfectly harmless— conventional notes thanking "Zenda" for a book or making some passing comment. It was the other half that were dynamite: these were much longer documents, written in a weird jargon in which code names were used (Roosevelt was "The Great One," Churchill "The Roaring Lion," Russia "The Tiger," etc.); international affairs were indiscreetly commented on; and strange matters were discussed, as how the writer cured himself of headaches at formal Senatorial dinners—a low opinion of Senators was indicated —by passing a Tibetan amulet over his forehead, and the mystic potency of certain symbols, including the Christian cross, the Mongolian lama's reliquary, and the Indian medicine man's charms (the Catholics would have not been pleased by such a juxtaposition). These letters, unhappily for the Republicans, were not on Wallace's letterhead (though the paper bore the Department's watermark), and they were signed not with his name but with two code initials.

The Republican National Committee bought the letters from "Zenda" and turned them over to two friendly newspaper publishers, Roy Howard and Paul Block, who assigned two of their best men to prepare a series of articles about the letters. The plan was to release the series, free, to every daily in the country. Roosevelt's health was generally known to be frail, nor did the Republican propagandists let the public forget his peculiar slip, just before the Democratic Convention, when he told the press that he hoped

Wallace would become "the next President of the United States." The Republicans thought the fear of an infidel crackpot becoming President might swing the election for them.

The Democrats heard about the letters more or less by chance—a fact which irritated Harry Hopkins, who was proud of the espionage network he had built up. *Why wasn't I told about this?* he exclaimed to friendly newspapermen. *I've got my people in every newspaper office in the country!* Like most of the Democratic chieftains, Hopkins took the "Zenda" threat very seriously. One of the few who refused to get ruffled was Roosevelt himself, who cracked, when Anna Rosenberg rushed down to Washington with the news: *Hell, couldn't we prove that Henry slept with the woman?*

The Rooseveltean intuition proved accurate. The delightful vision faded to a mirage before the Republicans' eyes. Howard backed out when his handwriting experts reported that, although the initials signed to the compromising letters (which were typed) resembled Wallace's handwriting, there was not enough to go on for a definite verdict. As a last resort, Block dispatched Ray Sprigle, of the *Pittsburgh Post-Dispatch,* to track down Wallace, who was then campaigning in the West, and ask him if the letters were genuine.* Getting wind of Sprigle's trip, the Democrats sent

---

* Curiously, no one, including the harassed Democrats, had thought of so direct an approach to the "Zenda" problem—perhaps because everyone assumed that Wallace had actually written the letters. Hopkins had set a special corps to reviewing every published word of Wallace, to see if the style and content of the "Zenda" letters harmonized with Wallace's previous lucubrations. The results were said to have been discouraging if not downright alarming.

out an emissary who got to Wallace first and doubtless gave him some good advice. When Sprigle arrived, Wallace laughed the whole thing off as an ancient hoax: *Are those things still kicking around? She's been trying to peddle them for years.* And that was the end of "Zenda."

GARLIC AND SOYBEANS

When Wallace became Secretary of Agriculture, he introduced into the Weather Bureau advanced methods of forecasting, including airplane observations and certain refined statistical methods he himself had worked out. At the same time, he was deep in correspondence with an Indian medicine-man who had pretensions as a rain-maker.

This kind of contradiction runs all through Wallace's personality. If mysticism attracts him, so does science— and especially that crudely materialistic and pragmatic kind of science which might be called "scientism." Mysticism and Scientism: the link may be that both approach life at a higher, or lower, level than the human; both are *impersonal* philosophies which seem to offer a way of bypassing the complexities and subtleties of human existence. Just as Wallace's mysticism is really *folk* mysticism, so he goes in for folk-scientific doctrines. His lifelong concern about diet is the most striking instance. One of the participants in the "Meet the Press" radio broadcast reproduced elsewhere in this book says that the one topic Wallace wanted to discuss, as they were sitting around waiting to go on the air, was not economic democracy or the atom bomb but his most recent discovery: the marvelous properties of garlic. Wallace is, in short, a "health crank"—a peculiarly Anglo-Saxon form of eccentricity. He is a vegetarian, a teetotaler, and, in his youth at least, an intrepid self-experimenter. At college, he went in for all kinds of stomach-turning regimens with the laudable purpose of finding a diet that would sustain human life for five cents a day. He was, unhappily, not successful. He tried living on nothing but rice, and got scurvy. He tried a diet of milk and popcorn, but found it unpalatable after a while. He tried a hideous goulash of soybeans, rutabagas, corn, and cottonseed meal, but lost heart after a week. He tried fasting, which at first produced splendid results; but he got hungry. At one point, his experiments laid him up in the hospital to recuperate.[61]

Another fad which Wallace cultivates is athleticism. He not only plays a fanatical game of tennis; he is also fond of Indian wrestling, volley-ball, squash, and even, if all else fails, plain setting-up exercises. He has made himself an expert in boomerang throwing, which, as the most dialectical of sports, since the starting-point is also the finish-line, fits in neatly with his personality. He always prefers to walk from the railroad station to his hotel, if possible carrying two heavy suitcases. There is sometimes an element of showing-off involved in Wallace's superman exhibitions, as when he refused a respirator during the high-level flight from Alaska to Siberia on his Far Eastern trip (he survived, to the astonishment of the others), or when, on one of his Latin American tours, he insisted on playing two sets of tennis as soon as he had arrived at Quito, the capital of Ecuador, a city of such elevation above sea-level that new arrivals find a short walk exhausting.

Some political and psychological speculations suggest

themselves. *Political*: Bernard Shaw * and Upton Sinclair come to mind as other instances of health-faddism among Leftists. It may be "no accident," as we used to say in the old days when things appeared simpler than they do now, that all three are highly uncritical of Stalinism. It may be that, in trying to reduce their own personal regimens to the simplest, most mechanical-materialist level, they exhibit a kind of shallow rationalism which is insensitive to human values and so can see in the Russian horrors simply a planned and rationalized society. There is something inhuman about health cranks, as there is something inhuman about the kind of people whose deepest emotions are stirred by animals. They try to solve the human tragedy at its lowest biological level, which is not different in kind from the "planning" methods of the Russian bureaucracy. *Psychological*: An element of masochism is perhaps involved in Wallace's dietary and athletic experiments; here, as in other aspects of his personality, a Freudian analysis might be interesting. Also is it not probable that, unable to bring his mental processes into effective order and harmony, Wallace finds an easy solace in controlling his digestion and his muscles?

Lack of interest in people seems to be accompanied by

---

* Who cabled the Kremlin, during the 1945 celebration of the anniversary of the 1917 revolution: "At the present time the Western states can learn and assimilate a great deal from Soviet Russia and themselves have nothing to teach her." And who sent the following message to his fellow-members of the Fabian Society on the occasion of the Society's diamond jubilee in the fall of 1946: "The only message I have for the moment is that the Fabian Society, having made Russia a great Fabian state, has now to make Wallace succeed Franklin Roosevelt as President of the United States."

a lack of human feeling: the man who has never shown much indignation about the brutalities of Stalin's regime will not hunt or fish because he hates to see animals die. A reporter once asked him what he considered the most important quality for a plant-breeder. His reply was unexpected—and shrewd: "Sympathy for the plant." [62]

"When Henry introduced me to boomerang throwing," Supreme Court Justice Jackson states, "I thought it was good fun and very interesting the way they came back, and that was enough for me. But not for Henry. He began by reading everything he could find on the history of boomerangs and their use among primitive tribes. Then he plunged into aerodynamics. . . . He had to find out *why* they act the way they do." [63] Wallace is as notably curious about *things*—his corn breeding, dietary experiments, and statistical work are examples—as he is incurious about *people*. In this latter category I include politics, in which, both as to theory and current events, he appears to be extraordinarily uninterested; at least, his ignorance of such matters as recent Marxist theory and elementary information about the Soviet Union is of such proportions as to make the assumption of lack of interest by far the most flattering to him.

7. A Man Divided Against Himself

HENRY WALLACE is not one man but two—and two people of such conflicting personalities that they would find it difficult to live inside the same house together, let alone inside the same skin. This is the key to his failure as a political leader, to his confusion in thought and ineffectiveness in action.

Henry Wallace No. 1 is a mystic, an amateur of esoteric doctrines, a man of profound moral convictions, an idealistic visionary whose eyes are fixed on a distant future, who shows a Hamlet-like indecision in action, and who lives only for great principles.

Henry Wallace No. 2 is an opportunist, adapting himself to the pressures of the moment, ready to foreswear his deepest convictions for immediate gain, a "practical politician," an extreme example of the American pragmatist, interested in "facts" rather than "theories," in statistics rather than values.

The coexistence of extremes in one personality is not damaging in itself: many temperaments derive their energy from the harmonized tension between extremes. But Wallace lacks the creative "middle term" which modulates between extremes and brings them into some kind of harmony. There is no connection between the two sides of his personality, so that *either* one *or* the other at any given moment expresses itself, but never a synthesis. Compromise is Wallace's substitute for synthesis, and he is genuinely surprised when it turns out to be an unacceptable substitute.

Lacking the psychological mechanism to modulate between values and action, the general and the particular, emotion and reason, and any number of other antinomies, Wallace can only alternately express the two sides of his nature, thinking one moment like a Tibetan seer and the next like a cost accountant, acting one moment like St. Francis of Assisi and the next like Boss Hague.

THE POLITICS OF CONTRADICTION

In his political utterances Wallace contradicts himself so frequently that it is the rule, not the exception.

He can achieve contradiction even in a single brief utterance. Three instances: (1) "No, I refuse to have the efficiency of the American farmer maligned, even though I know that he could do an almost infinitely better job than he does." [64] (2) "The Communists are the high priests of Materialistic Inevitability. I am always suspicious of anything labeled inevitable. . . . They [the common people] can bide their time; the inevitable swing of the pendulum will give them their opportunity." [65] (3) "The supreme freedom is the freedom of the people to know the truth. . . . For the peace and prosperity of the world, it is more important for the public to know the liberal truth than the reactionary truth. Perhaps some day all of us will be strong enough to stand the real truth." [66]

The reason for these contradictions is that Wallace always wants to get *everything* in: there are three mutually exclusive concepts of truth in the fifty-two words of the last quotation, for example. One of his former ghostwriters told me that Wallace was easy to work with except that he always wanted to repeat the whole book in each chapter; he seemed to dread exposing himself by making one point at a time. This compulsion becomes extreme in his final chapters, which are always in soft focus—fuzzy goodwill toward all men and everything in general, i.e., toward nobody and nothing in particular.

The note is struck in the preface to his earliest book, *Agricultural Prices* (1920): "I may say that I hold to no particular philosophy of economics. . . . One reason for the writing of this book is the belief that organized farmers and organized labor, working in conjunction with certain idealists, will make an effort to modify our present price-registering system. We are heartily in sympathy with such an effort, for the speculative system is far from perfect. But. . . ." There follows a demonstration that the speculative system, while not perfect, is pretty good. (A doctoral thesis could be written on the use of the word "but" in the writings of Henry Wallace.)

In *America Must Choose* (1934), Wallace proposes an economic policy for the United States. His argument: if we choose isolation and high tariffs, we will lose the farm export market and must withdraw fifty million acres of land from cultivation; if we go internationalist, we must lower tariffs enough to let in another billion dollars worth of imports, which will dislocate industry. His solution: split the difference—take twenty-five million acres out of production, let in half a billion exports. The pamphlet, precisely because, despite its title, it avoided a choice, pleased almost everybody and was the most popular thing Wallace wrote until his wartime speeches, which also pleased almost everybody. Charles A. Beard, however, was not pleased. In *The Open Door at Home* (1935), he wrote: "Wallace's program ... for agriculture is to force dislocations and readjustments in industry. ... Likewise, on their side, industrialists have shown themselves willing to dislocate agriculture. ... In other words ... politics is to continue as an open struggle among special interests, with what long-term outcome for the nation no one knows, although the present impasse in which such a struggle has eventuated is wellknown." On which Wallace commented: "I must confess it is a little disturbing to find Beard looking on my middlecourse proposal as special interest. It had seemed to me that the dislocations caused to agriculture and to industry were about even under this proposal." [67] Obtuseness could hardly go farther: Beard points out that a split-the-difference compromise between special interests is merely a form of the traditional pressure-group politics that have brought on the present dilemma; Wallace replies: but *both* parties are injured. Since his own personality is one in which clashing principles are never synthesized but merely given free rein against each other, Wallace applies the same rule to social problems. Paul Ward once noted: "Wallace ... has at bottom only two things to say: 'This hurts me more than it does you.' ... And: 'Two wrongs don't make a right, but they help a lot.' " [68] The same kind of thinking produced Wallace's spheres-of-influence policy last summer: let Russia dominate Eastern Europe, while we run Latin America. Out of these imperialist hunting-preserves will

come freedom for the oppressed; out of these two worlds
will come One World.

One of the most extraordinary of Wallace's books is *The
American Choice* (1940). Extraordinary because, even at
that late date, he still seems to think in isolationist terms;
there is none of that democratic-internationalist note stressed
in his later wartime speeches. Possibly the fact that Russia
was still allied to Germany was responsible. The most remarkable part of the book is the strategy it proposes for
dealing with Germany. This is simply to create a stronger
totalitarian empire than the Nazis. "We must at any sacri-
fice build up not only an armed defense but an economic
defense, both internal and in some part hemispheric, until
we are strong enough, economically and militarily, to do
business with Germany and its subject states, and to do that
business in a way that will be safe for us. . . . Against
Hitler's total warfare we must oppose a total defense. This
will involve sacrifices . . . conscription . . . the exactions
and restraints of an economy that . . . must become more
nearly self-contained and more closely subject to self-im-
posed controls. . . . Even if Germany wins, there is nothing
wrong about trading with a German-controlled Europe
after the war, so long as we conduct that trade in a way
which strengthens our American way of life and our national security." The formula for preserving "our American
way of life" is to imitate the Nazi form of life, but voluntarily and taking care to label it "democracy." "There is
possible a democratic self-discipline which serves the general
welfare but leaves free the soul of man. . . . This does not
mean that we must reconcile ourselves to regimentation. A

people may submit to laws and regulations of their own devising and still be joyous and free."

A year later, he was still trying to square the circle: to match the Nazis in totalitarian controls and discipline and at the same time "preserve American democracy." Thus in his Foreign Policy Association speech, on April 9, 1941, he proposed a Bill of Duties to accompany the Bill of Rights. Excerpts: "The Nazi youths are fighting with all their souls. Our youths must fight with even greater intensity. . . . The Nazi gradations of authority are imposed by fiat. Democracy, of course, also has gradations of authority, but the authority is derived from the free choice of the people. . . . The Nazis drive their people like cattle to the slaughter. [Cattle who are "fighting with all their souls," that is.—D.M.] The democracies, if they are to survive, must work out some way which, while holding fast to human rights, will at the same time permeate the individual souls with a feeling of responsibility so that the citizens of a democracy will be as willing to give wholehearted, unselfish service as the citizens of a totalitarian power."

During the war, Wallace, more than perhaps any other leader, justified the bloody struggle on the grounds of the splendid future victory would insure. But, when an interviewer asked him to define his postwar visions, Wallace shied off: "That's not a thing an executive should be thinking about these days. It's like a boy in the middle of a football game letting the dance that night take his mind off playing. We've got a war to win first." [69] Since Henry had been urging his teammates to win the game in order to hold the dance afterward, it was relevant to inquire whether the dance would be a success or—as it has turned out—a flop. But he was here clearly in his "executive," or B.E.W., mood; and as an executive he stressed the present and minimized the future, just as, in his role of "people's century" rhetorician, he reversed the process. This political dichotomy—and who but Wallace could throw himself so wholeheartedly into two such contradictory roles?—reflects a psychological split. Since for Wallace there is no integration between duty (the job, war) and enjoyment (play, peace), he suppresses his own personal drives and desires in order to play a public role. The divided man means the alienated man—alienated from his own spontaneous nature and from his fellows. Compare, for example, Wallace with another Common Man's friend: Gandhi. The one all abstract, vague, impersonal; the other concrete, sharp, personal. The one feeding us on windy generalizations, set speeches which correspond to his wholesale "planning" approach to people; the other's political prose style, like Tolstoy's, always precise, homely, concrete, dealing with personal interests. The one issuing marching orders for the Century of the Common Man; the other giving advice— as he has done in his fascinating weekly, *Harijan*—to a businessman who wants to be honest *and* successful or to a young woman whose virtue is besieged by Congress Party libertines. When Wallace wants people to do something, he makes a speech or writes a book; when Gandhi does, he does it himself—as in his campaign against the salt tax.

"A COLD FISH"

When Wallace was up for confirmation as Secretary of Commerce, several Senators voted against him just because they thought he was "a cold fish." They complained that

as Vice-President he had presided over them for four years
but that he had not tried to get to know them, nor had
he invited them into his office to "strike a blow for liberty,"
as had been the custom of his reactionary but genial predecessor, Cactus Jack Garner. This may appear a childish
reason for rejecting a cabinet member. As it may appear
trivial that Frank Kingdon, in his campaign biography
of Wallace, admits that his hero is incapable of small talk.
Or that, on Wallace's 1944 Far Eastern trip, he is said to
have kept aloof from his plane companions, never joining
in a drink (he doesn't drink, thank you) or a smoke (he
doesn't smoke, thank you), and brooding over his cracked
wheat in spiritual solitude; the result being that, after many
weeks of close contact, the whole company—diplomats, of-
ficers, and enlisted men alike—were heartily glad to see the
last of the Common Man's Friend.

It will be said that Wallace is just not "a good mixer,"
but I think it goes deeper. His shyness does not mask a
clumsy, inhibited warmth; it is rather the awkwardness
of a man confronted by something he neither understands
nor likes very well. And that something is people—the
Common Man, not generically but individually. This obtuseness has cost Wallace a lot in his political career; perhaps no other lack has been so damaging. He is constantly
getting involved with characters like Harold Young and
David Karr, whom he hopes to use to compensate for his
lack of understanding of people, but who turn out to be
catastrophic illustrations of that very lack. It is significant
that, when he left the Department of Agriculture, he did
not make any recommendations as to personnel to his successor. This was high-minded, but perhaps a little too high-

minded; perhaps it showed a lack of interest in the men he had worked with for eight years. When he took over the Department of Commerce, he took along with him only one major aide, the ineffable Harold Young. And, when he went to *The New Republic,* he left the selection of the editorial staff entirely to Straight.

Wallace loves humanity, but only *en masse;* he is interested in people, but only as units in statistical tables; the individual has to be raised to a higher power by multiplication before he "counts." Thus he does not read novels, plays, or poems; unless a book has footnotes and statistical tables, he suspects it is "a waste of time." One of his aides in Agriculture once tried to get him to read novels on the practical ground that they would show him how people "work" and so enable him to deal more effectively with them. Wallace agreed that he would like to be smarter about people, and he did read a few novels recommended by his aide. Not only was he bored, but he could not believe that they weren't "a waste of time" even for this utilitarian purpose. He went back to books with tables in them. "He has almost total recall on figures. Statistics are the most vivid part of a paragraph to him." [70]

It is remarkable how many men who have worked closely with Wallace and have "believed in him" feel let down, even betrayed. There is something abnormal, even monstrous, about Wallace's personality, they will tell you. He seems to be deficient not only in surface warmth but also in the deeper qualities of loyalty, affection, and sympathy which more intimate relationships demand. Men who have thought they could count on his friendship have found instead, when a test came, egotism and coldness. The friend of humanity in general turns out to be the friend of nobody in particular.

You can get an idea of what Henry lacks, a former close associate told me, *if you compare him with Jesse Jones. I had no use for Jones—he was a black reactionary, a man of extremely narrow intelligence. But, by God, when you finally pinned down the bastard, when you got him to agree to something, you knew he would stand by it, regardless of any pressure or afterthoughts. Now Henry was my kind of guy in every way—but you never knew when he was going to change his mind on you. You could trust Jones—once he committed himself, you knew where he stood. With Henry, you never really knew. And Jones never let down a subordinate. If you carried out his policies loyally, he would stick by you through hell and high water. As for Henry, well. . . .*

To which might be added, as a further indication of what Henry lacks and Jesse has, the observation which the latter once made to one of Henry's aides: *Whenever I want to get something out of Henry, I start off by telling him the dirtiest story I can think of. He hates it, and he gets so fussed that he gives me what I want just to get rid of me.*

"A MAN OF PAPER"

Just as Wallace thinks of people en masse, so he relates himself to them in terms of crowds, whether crowds physically present in a meeting hall or conceptually present as objects of the mass media of communication.

Unlike Hitler, Roosevelt, and other modern demagogues, Wallace is not adept at manipulating physical crowds.

Despite years of public speaking, he is still unable to project himself effectively or to dominate a living audience. Rather, his relation to such an audience is passive: he is "a sucker for applause"—or for booing. His mood soars or drops mercurially depending on the reaction of the crowd he is addressing. A comic instance occurred during the 1946 elections. On November 4, the eve of election day, Wallace gave three speeches for Mead in Brooklyn. The first was poorly attended (about four hundred), and the audience was listless; depressed, Wallace made political history by predicting the defeat of his own candidate: "I know that Senator Mead is not going to win." The second was big (thirty-five hundred) and lively; with engaging naïveté, Wallace told his audience that its enthusiasm had helped him shake off "that momentary fit of pessimism" and that he now was confident that Mead would win. The third was also big and cheerful, and again Wallace predicted victory. (It turned out his first premonition had been correct.)

Applause is essential to Wallace, perhaps because his image of himself needs constant reassurance. A hostile audience can cause him to change his speech as he goes along, as in the well-known case of the Madison Square Garden speech in the fall of 1946. A liberal leader has given, privately, a shrewd explanation of Wallace's partiality for the Communists, based on his own experiences at meetings sponsored by regular Democratic groups as against those sponsored by Stalinoid groups. When he speaks at the former, he says, no one pays much attention to him: "I sneak in, make my speech, am politely applauded, and sneak out again." But at Stalinoid meetings he feels like a

hero: a committee rushes down to conduct him tri-
umphantly to his seat on the platform; his speech is punctu-
ated by what the Russian press calls "stormy applause";
at the end there are cheers, and the whole audience rises in
tribute. "They certainly make you feel important." Evidently, Wallace falls heavily for this sort of thing.

It is with crowds as readers, and not as listeners, that
Wallace is effective. The French have an expression for the
kind of politician who writes a great deal in general but
does little in particular: *un homme de papier*. Wallace is
also a Man of Paper, emotionally feeding on paper phrases
(Economic Democracy, Full Employment, General Welfare, Common Man), nourishing his mind on paper statistics, using paper to insulate him from contact with human
reality. He himself is as much a victim of the illusion as
his liberal readers, habitually mistaking intentions for
achievements, words for actions. His *Sixty Million Jobs,*
for example, is a paper castle erected on two bits of campaign oratory by Roosevelt: the "Bill of Economic Rights"
which Roosevelt promulgated in 1944, a collection of
resonant (and, considering Roosevelt's own admission that
the New Deal was dead, cynical) banalities such as "the
right to a useful and remunerative job . . . the right of
every family to a decent home . . . the right to a good
education"; and the "postwar goal" of sixty million jobs,
which Roosevelt announced in his Chicago campaign
speech of October 28, 1944. This last so stirred Wallace
that he forgot the recent humiliations he had suffered, as
the last New Dealer, at Roosevelt's hands, and wired him:
YOUR GOAL OF SIXTY MILLION JOBS IS PERHAPS HIGH BUT I
GLORY IN YOUR DARING. AND AS YOU SAY AMERICA CAN DO THE

SEEMINGLY IMPOSSIBLE. The joke, of course, turned out to be that within a year of the close of hostilities, the economy was booming along at the rate of *over* sixty million jobs—and without any of the New Deal measures Wallace's book had insisted were essential to achieving the "daring" goal (by 1951, incidentally). Wallace's paper castle collapsed almost before the ink was dry on its pages. The final blow is the report by the Bureau of Census that in June, 1947, the number of civilian jobs alone (Wallace had figured in several millions in the armed forces) had, for the first time in United States history, topped sixty millions. And with a Right-wing Democrat in the White House and a Republican Congress! Even Henry Wallace must get a little discouraged sometimes.

HIS IMAGE OF HIMSELF

Henry Wallace is as distant from himself as from other people. The two things that appear to interest him most deeply and spontaneously are agricultural experiments and mystical doctrines. Yet he has suppressed both interests since 1933, when he went into politics, and, since he left the Department of Agriculture in 1940, he has not had even an administrative relationship to farming. A journalist asked him in 1942: "Do you think you would ever like to be an editor again?" "I like corn breeding better," he replied.[71] When I saw him at *The New Republic,* I asked him about this. "It's chicken breeding now," he answered, smiling. He carries on experiments at his farm in South Salem, New York, where he has 1,200 chickens on 124 acres. His aim is to get a hen that will lay eggs of uniform size; this will eliminate sorting and may prove to be even more profitable than the hybrid corn experiments. The farm is owned jointly with his sister, Mrs. Charles Bruggman, wife of the Swiss Minister to this country. After showing a visitor around the farm recently, Wallace observed, with a touch of wistfulness: "I often think what an attractive place this is for chickens. Good rains, not as cold as in Iowa in the winter and not as hot in the summer. . . . Being an editor is good fun, but occasionally you want to have some things you can touch." [72]

Some things you can touch: the phrase is revealing. Wallace is still part farmer, part laboratory scientist, and things aren't quite real to him unless he can "get his hands on them." Questions like the nature of World War II or the social character of the Soviet Union cannot be touched like chickens or settled with a slide rule like laboratory problems, and a temperament like Wallace's is helpless before them. So, like any other businessman with a hobby, he finds solace in weekends on his farm. But it would be as unthinkable to him as to the businessman to take this hobby "seriously"—although it is only in pursuing it that he feels secure and at home.

As for his mystical bent, that is little favored by his Stalinoid audience and so is firmly repressed. Henry Luce's magazines reflect all too accurately their proprietor's religious leanings, but Henry Wallace's magazine conforms to the irreligious canons of liberal journalism. Its symbol is not the mystic three dots within a circle which Wallace once adopted for his own sign, but a patriotic eagle-on-shield device which strikes the Lincolnesque note (it looks as though it came off a Civil War recruiting poster) required for the task at hand.

Even more than most political leaders, Wallace habitually suppresses any "merely" personal values, interests, or enjoyments in order to advance The Cause. It would never occur to him that a connection might be made between the two, or that it would be desirable to make it. This is why he appears so lumpish, even depressed, as he goes through his political paces, and why, although personally a kindly and well-intentioned man, he has frequently behaved in an unscrupulous way. Furthering The Cause means the building up of an image of himself as a Leader. Here the strands of egotism and altruism become intertwined beyond my ability to untangle them; the result is, however, clear enough: it is the precious image, the public face, which must always be preserved. At the time of the 1935 purge in Agriculture, one of the purgees asked him: *But, H. A.— why didn't you at least tell us about it in advance?* To which he replied: *I just couldn't face you.* One suspects that what Wallace couldn't face was not the suffering of his associates, but rather the shattering of his own image, in their eyes, as the great progressive. He is by no means a cold fish so far as this image is concerned: when it is threatened, his emotions are violent. When he left the White House after the most unexpected and brutal blow he has ever received—Roosevelt's abrupt dismissal of him from the B.E.W.—Wallace was in a state of hysterical collapse, weeping openly before the reporters. His emotions are cosmic-egotistical: he is cold toward individuals, but feels keenly his own sufferings. He feels them "objectively," so to speak: as the trials of the Messiah whom the Lord has chosen as his instrument of communication with the people.*

A GOOD MAN GONE WRONG?

The more charitable of Wallace's critics think he is a pathetic rather than a sinister figure, a man of decent instincts and intellectual ability who has been perverted by political life. I would agree with this, adding that, as noted above, it is Wallace's fallacious concept of politics—which in turn is connected with the neurotic conflicts within himself—which is mostly responsible for the damage. These conflicts disintegrate his own personality, so that he is constantly, without intending anything of the sort, betraying those who believe in him, running out on his own statements, and generally behaving in a way which, were it not so clearly the result of subconscious drives, one would be justified in calling cowardly and dishonest.

Since the major aim of this book is to consider Wallace as a political leader rather than as a personality, and since

* The image for which Wallace sacrifices himself and others shows itself quite literally. If one looks through a collection of newsphotos of Wallace, one finds that they fall into two contrasting categories: he is either wildly exhilarated, often with arm thrown high to an unseen crowd, in an embarrassing imitation of Roosevelt's confident grin; or else he is —apparently when the camera has caught him unprepared—as sodden and low-spirited as Hoover used to look. A friend who heard him speak at a recent luncheon notes that his usual expression was gloomy and depressed, but that he kept an eye out for the news-photographers and, when one was about to snap-flash, turned on a radiant smile quite unconnected with what he was saying. The effect was rather eerie. Thus the "public figure" becomes part of the news-gathering mechanism, playing the role of the dynamic, optimistic Leader as deliberately as any Hollywood character actor.

his political behavior has very little good to be said for it, the portrait drawn is doubtless blacker than a novelist, say, would draw. In some ways, then, let it be noted, Henry Wallace is an attractive and even admirable person—but let it also be noted that, politically, his virtues, since they are invariably negated by his approach to politics, only make him a more dangerous figure.

Here and there in his books there are passages which show a remarkable awareness of our modern dilemma, as: "I am convinced that behind economics, behind the economic machinery, there are certain truths in the field of philosophy—and behind philosophy in the field of religion—which have to do with the direction of the activities of man; and that these are more important at this stage of the game than economics itself. Unfortunately, because of their nature, it is impossible to evolve a body of facts which are subjected to critical analysis in this particular field." [73] Yet this is the man who, in politics, defends Russian totalitarianism as "economic democracy!"

When he is not making speeches, Wallace occasionally shows a knack for getting at the heart of things with shrewd humor. He complained about the dullness of Washington formal dinners: "Because, by protocol, the seating is ranked, you never get to meet any new folks." During the uproar in the press over the 1933 "murder" of the six million baby pigs, Wallace observed drily: "You'd think the farmers were raising those pigs for *pets*." And at the 1944 C.I.O. convention, where Murray introduced him with the line, "We love him because he is one of us, a common man," Wallace later (and privately) commented, after sharing a sumptuous luncheon with the C.I.O. top leaders:

"You common men live well." [74] But he would no more think of permitting this salty vein to crop up in the solemn wastes of his public utterances than he would go out without his pants.

There are even indications that Wallace has a sense of enjoyment. "I believe that most of us, once the opportunity is afforded, will discover within ourselves a variety of stimulating and pleasant things to do," he once wrote, listing "dreaming" as one of them.

8. The Mind of Henry Wallace

CLOSE-UP NO. 1

On January 16, 1947, I had a half-hour interview with Henry Wallace in his office at The New Republic. *His office is small, about the size of the other staff writers' offices there. He was writing on a pad with lead pencil when I came in; he was coatless, his hair was rumpled, he looked harassed and yet mild. His attitude throughout the interview was good-humored, unpretentious, shy, and friendly. I had come with my questions typed out on cards; I made notes on his replies. The following report is cast in a question-and-answer form, but it should be understood that Wallace's answers are not direct quotations but reconstructions based on my notes plus my memory, which is tolerably good in such matters.—D.M.*

Q.: In your first editorial in *The New Republic* you wrote: "Man must have freedom to learn the facts of the world he lives in and the right to speak about those facts. Those who deny this freedom have no part in the progressive movement." Do you think the Communists deny this freedom? A. (hesitantly): Yes, I suppose they do. Q.: Then would you favor their exclusion from the Progressive Citizens of America, which you lead? A.: Who told you I was a leader of the P.C.A.? That's not true—I have absolutely no connection with them! Q.: But you made the keynote speech at their founding meeting this fall. A.: Not

146

at all. I was there, and I gave them a talk, that's all. I'm not an officer of the P.C.A. I'm not even a member. Q.: Well, do you think Communists should be allowed in the P.C.A.? A.: How can you tell a Communist? What kind of litmus paper will you use? Rankin's, the Dies Committee's, the Department of Justice's? I don't want to go in for that kind of screening process. Q.: But suppose someone told you himself he was a Communist, what then? A. (after considerable fumbling around): Well, I think it would be undemocratic to discriminate against people just because they hold Communist beliefs.

Q.: You once called Marx's *Capital* the most influential modern book. What book has influenced your own thinking the most? A.: Where did you get that? I never said that. I think I once listed *Capital* among the hundred most influential books of our time, but I included a lot of others. *The Book of Mormon* was in there, too.*

Q.: What do you mean by "economic democracy"? A.: I've written a lot about that. But one thing I mean is a mixed economy—as much corporative, small business, co-operative, and government ownership as will produce the

---

* Wallace apparently was under the impression that to call *Capital* the most influential book was the same thing as saying he himself endorsed it. Thus, in his anxiety to dissociate himself from the Communists, he denied the statement. There is, however, evidence that he made it, or one very much like it, several times: (1) "He [Wallace] thinks Karl Marx's *Das Kapital* is the book that has most influenced the modern world." (Meyer Berger in *The New York Times*, November 6, 1940.) (2) At the *New York Times* 1937 Book Fair, Wallace was quoted as saying: "Whether we like it or not, everyone in the world today is different because of *Das Kapital*. Without *Das Kapital* there would have been neither the Communist nor the Fascist experiments." (*The New York Times*, November 5, 1937.)

most goods. I wouldn't allow strikes in government-owned plants—we can't go on having these tie-ups in basic industries; we've got to find some better way. Q.: What do you think of Lewis Corey's book on the mixed economy? A.: I don't know it. Who's Corey? Where does he teach?

Q.: You once stated that A.A.A. was an example of economic democracy because the farmers voted on all plans before they were adopted. Do you still believe this? A. (with more animation and confidence than at any other point in the interview): I think the A.A.A. was the nearest we've come in this country to real economic democracy. Q.: You've stated that we have political democracy while the Russians have economic democracy. But do the Russian people vote on the adoption of Five Year Plans? A.: We must avoid war with Russia. Nothing is more important now than peace between Russia and America. . . . We must be tolerant about Russia. . . . Q.: I can't see why you're so favorably impressed by the Soviet system. It seems to conflict with your own ideas and values. A.: You're probably one of those people who want war with Russia. (I denied this.) . . . When you look at Russia, you have to consider the historical background. Compared to what they had under the Czar, the Russian people are well off today. . . . Of course, I'm not a Communist. I'm an idealist, the Communists are materialists. . . . I wouldn't want communism over here, but it makes more sense in Russia.

Q.: Why does *The New Republic* call itself a progressive rather than a liberal magazine? A.: "Liberal" is too closely associated with the Manchester school of economics. . . . I have always preferred to call myself a progressive rather than a liberal. . . . I used to try to get President Roosevelt to use the term, "progressive," but he thought it was too closely connected with the Wisconsin movement. Q.: But in *Scribner's* for July, 1936, you rejected the nineteenth-century "idea of progress" and the "materialistic optimism" that went with it. Yet you call yourself a progressive. A.: I must have been thinking of the way businessmen talk about progress. There's a difference between progress and progressivism. Q.: What is the difference? A.: Well, for one thing (long pause) . . . Of course, sometimes I get into a mood of wondering what it's all for. Sixty million jobs—but what do we do after that?

Q.: What is your position on universal peacetime military training? A.: I'm against it. Q.: Do you think Truman should grant an amnesty to all conscientious objectors? A.: Yes.

Q.: Do you think the ration for German civilians should be raised to two thousand calories? A.: Only if they don't get more than other countries are getting. Q.: What is your opinion of the Potsdam agreement—is it too severe, not severe enough, or about right? A. (After some hesitation): I don't believe I've ever written anything about that. Guess I have no opinion for publication on that. Q.: What do you think about the prohibition against sending books and magazines to Germany? A.: Well, I don't know. I think you'd have to be on the scene to have an intelligent opinion. I wouldn't want to criticize the policy of the Army on that without knowing more about it. Q.: What did you think about Byrnes's Stuttgart speech last September? A.: Byrnes at Stuttgart? I don't recall any such speech.

CLOSE-UP NO. 2

*On January 10, 1947, Henry Wallace took part in the
weekly "Meet the Press" program presented by the Mutual
Broadcasting System in cooperation with* The American
Mercury. *His interviewers included Marquis Childs and
Lawrence Spivak, editor of the* Mercury. *The following
excerpts are taken from Mutual's transcript of the broadcast
—D.M.*

Q.: I wonder what you think about Secretary Byrnes's
conduct of our foreign policy. A.: I have never said anything about Secretary Byrnes's conduct of the policy, favorable or unfavorable, and don't intend to say anything
favorable or unfavorable now. Q.: Mr. Wallace, wasn't your
Madison Square Garden speech interpreted that way? A.:
Yes, but Secretary Byrnes wasn't in my mind when I made
that speech. . . . Q.: One thing we have all been curious
about is, why did you omit some of the parts of your speech
that had been critical of Russia after you had been booed?
A.: Because I felt I had been booed enough. I didn't see any
particular point in making a riot there. . . .

Q.: Do you think President Truman could be renominated in 1948? A.: I assume he will be renominated. Q.:
In that case, sir, do you have any political ambitions?
Would that mean that you think there would have to be
a third party formed in which you could carry them out?
A.: I don't see how anybody nominated by a third party
could realize any ambition. . . . But I do know that we
have to end as soon as possible the one-party system that we
have in the United States at the present time. I think we've
got to return to the two-party system. . . . Q.: You are not

for a third party? A.: Not unless it is necessary in order that we may have a genuine two-party system. If there is going to be a conservative Democratic Party and a conservative Republican Party, obviously there will have to be a third party in order to kill off one of the old parties. We can't have two conservative parties. . . . Q.: Mr. Wallace, I was interested in your reference to the one-party system. It has now been about four months since you left the Truman administration. What is your opinion of the Truman administration and its position today? A.: I was exceedingly pleased by the economic report submitted by the President the day before yesterday. . . . I also wrote an editorial commenting very favorably on the nomination of General Marshall for Secretary of State. Those two events seemed to me to strengthen the position of the Administration very materially. Q.: How does that jibe with your statement that we have a one-party system running the country today? A.: Well, possibly that remark can more characterize my feeling of two days ago than it does today.* I will grant that I haven't brought all my thinking quite completely up to date there. I did feel that way very strongly up until the day before yesterday. Q.: Does that mean that you have left the Democratic Party? A.: It does not mean that. That is some of the false propaganda which has been going around the country. Q.: Well, if there is only one party now, what difference does it make which party you belong to? A.: I referred to this bipartisan policy which is being advocated in certain quarters. I certainly don't think it characterizes the great bulk of the members of the Democratic

* Two minutes ago, rather. See above.—D.M.

Party in this country. I don't think they feel that way at all. . . .

Q.: Mr. Wallace, don't you think that the Communists, no matter how small a minority they are of any organization, are a disturbing influence, that they are anti-democratic? A.: Oh, sure; I agree with you on that. Q.: Well, why would you want them in any progressive movement? A.: I am not saying I want them in any progressive movement. Who said I wanted them in any progressive movement? Q.: Well, you spoke a minute ago— A.: If you allow that little thing to dominate your mind, it means that you have become a Red-baiter, a person who wants to sic the F.B.I. onto your neighbor; it interferes with everything you want to do, to do a job in the field of progressive activity here. It is just exactly what the enemy wants to see happen. I refuse to allow that to become a dominating consideration in my mind. Q.: What "enemy," Mr. Wallace? Who is the enemy? A.: The reactionaries.

Q.: Mr. Wallace, on May 8, 1942, you said: "This is a fight between a slave world and a free world. Just as the United States in 1862 could not remain half slave and half free, so in 1942 the world must make its decision for complete victory one way or the other." Don't you think that thing still holds true today, and that we are fighting against a slave world? A.: I do not think that. Q.: You think Russia is a free world? A.: I do not think Russia is a free world, but I do not think it is a slave world in the way I meant in 1942 and in the way you mean today. If I agreed with you, I would know that we have to fight now. Fortunately, I don't agree with you. I am sorry that you feel it is necessary to start a war against Russia today, and if you want to deny that, go right on the air now and deny that you want a war with Russia today. Q.: I deny that I want a war with Russia today. A.: I am glad I heard you deny it. . . .

Q.: Mr. Wallace, were you in favor of appeasement of the Nazis? A.: I certainly was not. Q.: I know you were against the aggressive actions of Hitler. Why do you now apologize for or explain away the aggressive actions of the Russians? A.: Because I think they are of a different nature altogether. Q.: Isn't aggression aggression, no matter what the nature is, so far as the people who are taken over are concerned? Do you think the Poles think that the aggressive action against them is any different than the Czechs thought when Hitler took them over? A.: I think it is quite a different situation at the present time. Q.: Will you explain what the difference is, Mr. Wallace? A.: I think it would take a very long time to explain, and I think there would be grave misunderstanding caused over the air if we started on that long path of explanation. . . .

CLOSE-UP NO. 3

On April 28, 1947, Wallace held his first press conference after his return from his European tour. It was largely devoted to his complaints that the press had "misquoted" or "incompletely reported" what he had said on that tour. The conference itself, however, provided the explanation of why the press has such difficulty getting Wallace's ideas straight. The following account is taken from a story by Bert Andrews in The New York Herald-Tribune *of May 3.—D.M.*

This Washington session was not "incompletely reported." There was, in fact, a transcript made by a shorthand writer. Some of it will be reproduced here to show how the extemporaneous remarks of Mr. Wallace look when reduced to writing.

The partial transcript will be prefaced by:

1. A statement, which can be made without fear of contradiction by anyone who was at the press conference, except perhaps Mr. Wallace, that the reporters, one and all, had some difficulty in following him.

2. A statement, which can be made under the same terms, that most of the reporters believe Mr. Wallace would be very well advised to settle for a few misquotations, rather than to have his off-the-cuff remarks quoted exactly as made.

3. That the reporters, one and all, believe Mr. Wallace would be still better advised if he would confine his public utterances to speeches prepared in advance and read by him as they are written, with due attention paid to periods and commas and other punctuation marks.

4. That, after the press conference was over, the reporters present were inclined to be charitable to their colleagues abroad if they did indeed misquote Mr. Wallace on the matter of "ruthless imperialism."

Q.: "Would you care to elaborate on your statement that this country should lend fifteen or seventeen billion dollars to Russia?"

A.: "I might say with regard to that . . . that the . . . that the . . . the thing came up in informal conversation with the members of the French Chamber of Deputies. In general conversation it came up about the difficulties with the Moscow Conference and what might be done to establish peace.

"That is how it originated and at that point—well, I had also discussed as a separate point the need for developing the backward areas of the world and taking care of the reconstruction of the devastated areas and indicated that it would amount for that program over a period of five years . . . the need might be between . . . somewhere in the neighborhood of fifty billion dollars.

"That was one segment.

"The other segment was the difficulty of the Moscow Conference, and at that stage I indicated that Russia's devastation was probably greater than any other place, partly because of the drought, partly because of the devastation. There were at least thirty million in Byelo-Russia and the Ukraine who live under the most difficult situations. . . . That Russia had to do something for those people and that they were taking it out of Germany's hide, but in the process the results might be to make Germany into a plague spot.

"The only place where adequate supplies were available was the United States, which I recognize at the present time it is politically impossible to get goods from for Russia now, but later there will be a surplus and at that time the picture might change.

"I went on and on describing that and trying to analyze the economic picture. It was presumably off the record. The press wasn't there, but we know how those things leak. A few hours later The Associated Press and The United Press inquired if it was true that I favored a seventeen-billion-dollar loan to Russia. I had mentioned no figure whatever, and I immediately knocked the story down. I did not give any figure.

"The International Bank for Reconstruction should consider the entire question. And I still think definitely, so far as the general impression is concerned, I don't think it makes any difference. I still think that a very large loan to Russia at low interest rates is necessary. I also said I thought the need of Poland was very great, and the need of Greece, that they all need help."

Q.: "What criticisms do you have of Russia?"

A.: "I have made those criticisms repeatedly. I stated that Russia should have joined the International Bank for Reconstruction, that she should have joined the Food and Agriculture Organization, that she should have joined U.N.E.S.C.O., that she should have displayed a greater confidence toward the United Nations than she has. I have always criticized Russia, but that is never news. Apparently it falls between the situation . . . between the man and the dog. One is news and the other is not. I have spoken for free enterprise capitalism. It has never appeared in the press."

Q.: "Do you think there is a fundamental difference?"

A.: "It is parametric more than fundamental. I also mentioned that only four Russians—I don't know about this myself but I was told by reliable authorities—are employed in the secretariat of the United Nations, whereas there are some two hundred and sixty Americans and one hundred British and sixty or seventy others. I think that is parametric, too."

(Webster's definition of "parameter": 1. Math. A. An arbitrary constant characterizing by each of its particular values some particular member of a system of expressions, curves, surfaces, functions, etc. B. A variable through functions of which may be expressed other variables, as the co-ordinates of a locus. C. In conics, the third proportional to any diameter and its conjugate, or in the parabola, to any abscissa and the corresponding ordinate. Webster's definition of "parametric": Of or pertaining to, or in terms of, a parameter.)*

* To which may be added the following comments, for which I am indebted to another reporter who was present at the interview: "After Wallace had condemned the witch hunt for 'Reds' among Government employees, I said that his sentiments were very fine but didn't he recognize that, in addition to being a Left-wing political party, the American Communist Party is also part of a fifth column whose concern is not peace but Russian strength? He replied: 'I am not an expert on communism in the United States. So far as I know, I've seen only two Communists here. I don't know whether the Communist Party follows the Moscow line or not.' Later, after he had said he condemned Russian as well as American imperialism, I asked if he knew of any specific examples of Russian imperialism. 'Well, no, not offhand.' Then another fellow asked him if he didn't think that Russia's interest in the Dardanelles and Turkey's border provinces was imperialism. He said that, so far as he knew, Britain, America, and France had agents operating in the Near East. 'It is simply the result of a vacuum being left there at the end of the war. As for the Dardanelles—even the Czars wanted them, so you can hardly call that imperialism.'"

9. The Political Meaning
of Henry Wallace

I

WALLACE is an advertising man's Messiah. This means two things:

(a) Since the citizens of a mass society have no way of knowing the effect on their own interests of the policies of a Leader, it is possible to create an image, an eidolon, which promises all things to all men and delivers some things to those in control. Wallace is the product of the people who have manipulated him, skillfully "built him up," written his speeches for him: yesterday, certain New Deal cliques; today, the Stalinoids. The imposture deceives even those who work it. I talked with one of the men Wallace "purged" from Agriculture in 1935. Shamefacedly, he confessed that, despite this personal knowledge of the man's quality, he had done his best to get him the vice-presidential nomination at the 1944 Democratic convention. "I worked like a dog for Wallace at Chicago. Damned if I know why now. You get a picture going of what a guy is and you get hooked with that picture." Such illusions die hard. How many liberals—not the rank-and-file readers and listeners, but the insiders, the boys in the know—have been hooked by the picture of Wallace they themselves created? The process goes farther: it is a reasonable surmise that Wallace is also "hooked" by the synthetic public image his manipulators have made of him, i.e., that he believes his own propaganda. This is more common than is generally realized.

(b) If this type of Messiah alienates others from their private, personal—hence real—interests and values, it is not to impose *his* values. In fact, a double alienation takes place. The advertising man's Messiah comes to the people not with an image of his own convictions but with a mirror reflecting what the masses want to see—or rather—what they have been conditioned by the existing culture to want to see. There are other images—of fraternity, spontaneous enjoyment, liberation, rebellion—to which people would also respond, with more difficulty; but those in control of society. whether as industrialists, trade-union leaders, or government officials, have every reason to prefer the image built up by our culture as it now exists. A true popular leader would use these more difficult appeals in order to destroy the status-quo culture. He would try to arouse similar feelings in others by expressing his own fraternal, rebellious values. The demagogue, however, suppresses his own spontaneous personality just as Hollywood moviemakers suppress theirs, and for the same end: to mirror mass tastes. To lead, he follows.

2

Since he denies his own personal values, he is insensitive to those of others. Wallace's favorite political concept, that of the Common Man, shows this quite clearly—all the more so since it is an attempt to demonstrate quite the opposite.

"It directly follows from Wallace's terms," David T. Bazelon notes, "that men must *become* 'common' if they are not already so, before they can be united. That is, if in themselves or their conditions of life they happen to have distinguishing characteristics, these must be ignored for political purposes (and, with the mechanization of culture, eventually for *all* purposes—including the vision of self). . . . The 'common man,' moreover, is to be considered only as a consumer in industrial society—not even as producer, which role is infinitely more significant. In the end, if men actually come to see themselves as common, society will contain not men at all, but just so many parts of the total supply of refrigerators, potatoes, newspapers and movie seats. . . . Now to be a mere consumer demands nothing of the *person*—he is given things, his role is passive. If you are without fault, if you are common—you will be given what you need to exist, including a 'job.' The notion of the common man can be summed up: become like everybody else, become nothing. This is a long way from the Western concept of the citizen. One wonders what grandfather 'Uncle Henry' would have made of Henry III's creature." [15]

3

One wonders indeed. As noted in the first part of this article, Uncle Henry was a real person, not an advertising agency's eidolon. There is pathos in Wallace's own recognition of this difference. "Grandfather was a great and strong man," he remarked on one occasion. And on another: "We modern Wallaces are a dull lot. You must feel like crawling under the carpet when you see me coming."

4

As a Messiah, Wallace's view of political issues is simple: all those who are with him are good, all against him are bad. This approach gives him and his followers a warm moral glow, but it also prevents them from understanding much. "He was apt to view clashes of economic forces," reminisces George Peek, "as struggles between good men and bad men and not as between groups all of whom believed that right was with them. Since Henry was always with the good men, he never quite got the whole of any picture. He believed in low tariffs, for instance, as a moral issue." [76] This tendency to throw a cloak of morality over practical politics—an art in which Wallace has little to learn from either the nineteenth-century British empire builders or their twentieth-century Russian successors—used to cause intense discomfort to the clear-minded Rexford Tugwell. *Henry's worst trait*, Tugwell once remarked, *is his habit of rationalizing, as direct messages from God, the dirty deals and compromises that all politicians must engage in*. During the A.A.A. period, when Wallace was intensely disturbed about the sabotage of production he had to carry out, someone suggested that now the farmers would have leisure to develop their personalities and to play with the kiddies, as well as "more time for reflection, books, music, travel, sociability, and even art." "Wallace fired up to that. 'That is fine. It is true. We must make a religion of that!' Tugwell gave forth a sort of muted groan. 'My God, Henry, no!' he said earnestly. 'Rationalize it any way we have to, we can't make a religion out of growing or making fewer goods with this whole country and the whole world in bitter need.' " [77]

5

Wallace's chief political appeal is probably this moralistic approach. People feel a very deep need to make a connection between moral values and political issues. In the past two centuries this connection has been made, on a historically significant scale, first by the eighteenth-century liberals and then by the socialists and anarchists. Today, however, the connection has been broken: the movements that formerly established it have either dwindled to historical insignificance or else have become debased; nor has any new movement with popular appeal arisen to make a fresh connection between ethics and politics—at least not in the West. In this country today there is not one mass party or movement which conceives of politics as anything except a technique of getting power. The secret of Wallace's political vitality is that he exploits demagogically the need for a "moralized politics."

6

In the decadence of American "Left" politics, Wallace brings everything to a loud discordant finale. His published utterances are a jumbled medley of every popular tune since 1890: the populist anti-Wall-Street tradition; the twin myths of the Farm Boy and the middle-class Free Enterpriser à la Horatio Alger; the industrial unionism of the C.I.O.; the state-capitalist ideas of the New Deal; and the two great international myths of our time: Soviet Collectivism and the War to Make the World Safe for Democracy. In this jangle of old and new ideologies, the rising ones drown out the dying ones, so that Wallace, without any conscious effort on his part—consciousness is not his strong point—has gradually come to orient his politics around the last two. And now that American liberals are confronted with a disharmony between the Soviet myth and the War for Democracy myth, so blatant that even Wallace cannot play both tunes at once, he has been driven to a choice—and has chosen the former. He continues to fiddle away hopefully on all strings, of course: on his recent European trip, which sealed his commitment to the Soviet myth, he arrived in England with ten dozen eggs from his Katonah farm for British poultry breeders. ("You take three inbred Leghorn whites and three Rhode Island reds, crossbreed them, and you have excellent eggs," he explained on disembarking from the plane.) And in Paris he kept insisting, perhaps a bit nervously, that he was just a simple American free-enterpriser. But his fortissimo is reserved for other themes. Such grace notes are more and more smothered by the dominant chords of Soviet imperialism.

7

He is well fitted for the role he has assumed of late years: to overlay with Common Man rhetoric such unpleasant features of modern life as war and totalitarianism. Lacking in his own personality any connecting tissue between theory and practice, ideal and reality, he is incapable of a critical view: that is, of comparing what he wants with what he gets.* Nothing discourages him, nothing dis-illusions him. He is incapable of losing faith, since he takes it as a matter of course that "ideals" exist on one plane and "reality" on another. Thus it is logically impossible for him to draw conclusions from the failure of the one to harmonize with the other.

8

In 1936, he wrote: "The power over nature given by science and invention during the nineteenth century was so great that the idea of 'Progress, Unending and Unlimited' was born. . . . The nineteenth century gave man a ma-terialistic optimism which was bound to disappear the moment the nations found it necessary to live with each

---

* A critical approach disturbs him profoundly, as in his comment on Veblen, whom he admired—or rather, wanted to admire—greatly: "Un-fortunately, Veblen rarely tried to find a constructive solution. He was satisfied for the most part with analysis. . . . I think there is far more possibility of good in the American businessman than Veblen cared· to admit. Since 1915, many of our businessmen, notably the DuPonts, have shown a willingness to put exceedingly large sums of money into scientific research." He might have added that our businessmen have also shown their virtue by paying out billions of dollars in wages, not to mention the splendid support they have given our railroad system—essential to the Common Man's welfare—by paying freight charges. He might also have noted that the DuPonts' post-1915 (significant date!) research ex-penditures were largely in the munitions field. Not that this would seriously worry him. "The war," he observed in 1942, "the war has brought forth a new type of industrialist who . . . has caught a new vision of opportunities in national and international projects. He is willing to cooperate with the people's government in carrying out socially de-sirable programs. He conducts these programs on the basis of private enterprise and for private property while putting into effect the people's standards as to wages and working conditions. We shall need the best efforts of such men as we tackle the economic problems of peace."

other. . . . The illusion of . . . unlimited progress is now being demonstrated."

In 1945, he wrote: "We, too [like the Victorians], live in an age of incessant progress, and the horizon is much brighter with opportunity than Lord Macaulay could possibly have envisioned for his England of a century ago."

Why did he change his mind? Not because the events of the intervening decade afforded any ground for optimism about "incessant progress" but, on the contrary, because they were so horrible that pessimism became dangerous to his faith as a liberal. Thus the doubt-ridden reformer of 1936 became, by the curious dialectics of the situation, the exultant ideologue of the People's Century. The absence of any grounds for optimism, perhaps even hope, forced the development of a factitious optimism which suggests that euphoria characteristic of the "high" stages of manic depression. Henry Wallace's psychological degeneration (perhaps disintegration?) in the last decade is more than a personal tragedy; a similar devolution can be traced in the American liberal-labor movement generally.

10. To Be Continued in Our Next

IT IS RISKY to write the life of any man before he is
dead. The perils are especially great in the case of Henry
Wallace, an unstable personality in an unstable period.
At the moment of writing this final chapter, in the late fall
of 1947, Wallace's future is as vague as his prose style. On
the one hand, those tender shoots of hope for a third party
which sprouted last spring have by now withered: it appears most unlikely that Wallace will run for President
next year. On the other, the political experts have read
funeral services over Wallace at least three times of late
years: after he failed to get the Vice-Presidency in 1944,
after he was forced out of the administration in 1946, after
his European tour last spring. Each time, the obsequies
turned out to be premature. This is less a tribute to Wallace's political vitality than a symptom of the anxiety which
many Americans feel about the world in which they live.
Wallace can make political blunders; he can make speeches
and write articles which are masterpieces of confusion,
equivocation, and contradiction; he can identify himself
with the Communists—but so long as he remains a symbol
of hope and of dissidence, so long will he retain a mass
following.

RETURN OF THE NATIVE

Soon after he returned from Europe last May, Wallace
set out on a speaking tour of the country under the auspices

of the Progressive Citizens of America. To every one's surprise, including his own, the trip was a great success. Large audiences turned out to hear him and even paid for the privilege: twenty thousand in Chicago at from $.60 to $2.40 a ticket (plus another $10,000 in contributions to P. C. A. from the audience); twenty-five thousand in Los Angeles, at a $3.60 top; ten thousand University of California students, who cut classes to attend an open-air meeting after he had been refused the use of any college building; ten thousand in Washington, D. C., who paid an average of $2.00 a ticket; etc. Considering that Wallace had just returned from a trip abroad during which he had violently assailed his own country's policies and praised with equal warmth those of Britain and Russia, this popular reaction was unexpected. One explanation may be that in our culture the cynical press agent's motto is valid: any publicity is good publicity. The European tour had yielded Wallace more headlines than anything in his previous career. Many people must have turned out to hear Wallace for the same reason they eat Wheaties and smoke Camels: because they had seen his name in print so much. That the press comment was unfavorable was either beside the point or else actually in Wallace's favor. There must be millions of readers who are, with reason, so suspicious of the big-circulation press that they assume that any idea or personality attacked by it must be on *their* side. As in the case of Roosevelt, the hostility of the press may be one of Wallace's political assets.

But the main reason people turned out in such numbers to listen to Wallace was, I think, summed up by Morris Rubin at the time: "Henry Wallace has become for the

moment the man in America who symbolizes the deep-
going frustration and insecurity which so many Americans
feel as they contemplate the domestic and international
scene. Wallace's greatest appeal, it seems to us, lies somewhat less in the fact that he has a 'program' . . . than in
the fact that, being footloose politically and fancy-free ideo-
logically, he can and does strike out in all directions and
against all groups in power in the United States, whether
Democrats in the Administration or Republicans in control
of Congress." [80] In short, Wallace appears to most of those
who listen to him sympathetically not as a leader in action,
but as an embodiment of a mood. It is a mood which is not
critical because it is too desperate to afford criticism: it
accepts Wallace on his own valuation as a lover of peace
who is trying to find a way to avoid World War III.

DOLDRUMS

The unexpected success of his speaking tour created in
Wallace a state of euphoria which has lasted up to the present. His editorial comments in *The New Republic* turned
into lengthy accounts of his triumphal progress, written
with the expansiveness of a Messiah who has at last made
contact with his followers. If his editorials in the first
months of the magazine were clumsy exercises in Wallesian
generalities, his more recent efforts have been as detailed
and garrulous as a letter to the folks back home. A considerable pomposity has also crept into them; they are letters
home, but letters written by a Senator. For example:

"During a 10-day trip in New England, I saw that section of our country turn in color. The autumn foliage in the
Berkshires, Vermont and New Hampshire made the fall

visit a thing of beauty. Surpassing the natural beauty was
the heartening attitude of thousands of New Englanders on
the grave problems of the day. Here, as elsewhere, there is
concern about the course of our present foreign policy and
the failure to take steps which will either avert or cushion
the oncoming depression. Provost Paul Buck of Harvard,
expressing his disagreement with some of my views, still
came to the Soldiers' Field meeting. . . ." [81]

It is sad to report that, despite the heartening attitude of
thousands of New Englanders, things have not been going
at all well with Wallace of late. The brute realities of politics in our day cannot be overcome by any number of
speeches and rallies, even rallies which number among the
audience Provost Paul Buck of Harvard. For many months,
Wallace has had no front-page headlines and very few in-
side-page stories. On both the domestic and the foreign-
policy front, the Truman Administration appears to have
stolen his thunder, leaving him in a "me, too" position,
which is an intolerable attitude for a Messiah.

At home, Truman's veto of the Taft-Hartley bill has
swung labor once more behind the Administration—which
is one more indication of the modest political ambitions of
our labor movement. Internationally, the Marshall Plan has
similarly undercut Wallace's position, since it proposes precisely what he had long been calling for: a broad program
of economic aid to Europe without the military emphasis
of the Truman Doctrine. Last July, he was forced to come
out publicly in support of the Marshall Plan as "what I
have been advocating all along." And when, a few weeks
later, Russia committed the tactical blunder of withdrawing
from the Plan and forcing her satellites to do likewise, Wal-

lace had to criticize the action. Ever since, he has been in a dilemma: on one hand, his ties to the Communists are too close (and his whole way of thinking about world events has been too thoroughly shaped with a pro-Russian bias) for him to make a break with Russia and to press for the Marshall Plan; on the other hand, since the Plan is remarkably similar to what he has been advocating for a long time, he cannot openly attack it. The result has been a paralysis and a flight into themes like the beauty of the New England autumn—and even a literal flight. His tour of Palestine in October was such an escape: here was one part of the world where the U.S.A. and the U.S.S.R. were in agreement. Whereas he had gone to Europe last spring to preach a dramatic—and indeed explosive—doctrine on foreign policy, his trip to Palestine was made "to see whether in any way my knowledge of agriculture and industry would tend to facilitate the cause of peace in the Near East." Soil erosion and a T.V.A. for the Jordan valley are respectable topics of liberal speculation, but they could hardly be expected to produce headlines. Nor did they. But headlines were perhaps the last thing Wallace wanted at the moment, caught as he was between the Marshall Plan and the increasing aggressiveness of Russian policy.

At this writing, Wallace's political fortunes are in the doldrums. The trade wind of Stalinism has died down, and no other winds have come up to fill his sails. There was a time not so long ago when a third party, built around Wallace as a 1948 presidential candidate, seemed to be in the making. Almost every week, Wallace would come out with a threat to "take a walk" if the Democratic Party did not reform and become a "people's peace party." On June 5 last, he was asked whether he would support Truman for re-election. "That depends," he replied—and then, after a moment's hesitation, "I would say, no." The labor movement, however, has shown increasingly less interest in a third party since Truman's veto of the Taft-Hartley bill. The *coup de grâce* was struck by President Whitney of the Brotherhood of Railroad Trainmen when he came out for Truman's re-election on the grounds that his Taft-Hartley veto had "vindicated him in the eyes of labor" and had shown the "fundamental liberalism of the Democratic Party." Since Mr. Whitney's union, after Truman broke the 1946 railroad strike, had voted a special $2,500,000 fund to defeat Truman in 1948, and since Mr. Whitney himself has for years been close politically to Wallace, his defection was a serious, and probably a fatal, blow to Wallace's presidential hopes.

HENRY AND THE U.S.S.R. (CONTINUED)

More than ever, Wallace's significance in American politics is that of the outstanding apologist for Russian foreign policy. His closest associates and advisers continue to follow the Stalinoids. The result is his present "line" on foreign policy: that the U.S.A. and the U.S.S.R. can get along together if neither gets "tough"; that each should work within the United Nations and not go off on its own imperialist tangent. This seems to many sincere people to be an impartial policy which will promote world peace. Actually, it is an *ad hoc* policy, adopted after Byrnes's Stuttgart speech in the fall of 1946 had signalized a stiffening of

American resistance to the aggressive tactics of the Kremlin. During the first year after Potsdam, when it was *Russia* that was being tough, when it was *Russia* that was wrecking the United Nations by obstructive vetoes, when it was *Russia* that was taking the diplomatic offensive everywhere —in that period, Wallace showed no public concern about this aggression. On the contrary, even then his counsels of moderation and restraint were directed almost exclusively at the Anglo-American bloc. Thus a speech of his before the Women's National Democratic Club on March 19, 1946, was summarized by *The New York Times:* "He declared that if the United States and Britain 'try to strut around the world and tell people where to get off,' they will be 'put off' the globe." And three days later, he indignantly demanded that, in the interests of harmony with Russia, American troops should be withdrawn at once from Iceland. There is no record during this period, however, of his having shown equal concern over Russian troops in Eastern Europe. Up to the fall of 1946, Wallace objected to such feeble resistance as the United States made to Russian demands as injurious to the idea of One World. When his own country finally counterattacked, he changed his line to the defensive concept of Two Worlds, with Russia being left alone in her World; this shift was precisely geared to a similar change in Russian foreign policy.

The result has been that, in the last eighteen months, Wallace has isolated himself more and more not only from the Democratic Party but also from the liberal-labor movement. The formation in January, 1947, of Americans for Democratic Action was the most significant split in that movement that has occurred in many years. It was a direct re-

tort to the union, a few days earlier, of the National Citizens
Political Action Committee and the Independent Citizens
Committee of the Arts, Sciences and Professions * into the
Progressive Citizens of America, with Henry Wallace as
their chief spokesman. The only issue separating A.D.A.
from P.C.A. is the Russian issue: P.C.A., like its parents,
N.C.P.A.C. and I.C.C.A.S.P., is firmly controlled by the
Stalinoids; A.D.A. is not only critical of Russian foreign
policy but also bars Communists from membership. The
interesting thing is that A.D.A., the newcomer, has attracted
practically all the "big" liberal names, from Mrs. Roosevelt
to Leon Henderson and Chester Bowles, and including a
half-dozen top trade-union leaders. Also including Harold
Ickes, who accepted the chairmanship of I.C.C.A.S.P., pooh-
poohing friends who warned him it was Communist controlled, and who quietly resigned in the fall of 1946 after
several unhappy experiences had convinced him that the
warnings had been accurate. It has taken the liberals a long
time to learn the facts of life about Stalinism—the present
clash between American and Russian national interests has
wonderfully speeded up the process—but they seem to be

* For Wallace, as for many others, these two groups were important
"transmission belts" to the Communist apparatus. C. B. ("Beaney") Bald-
win, executive head of N.C.P.A.C. and a former top aide of Wallace's in
Agriculture, is a prominent fellow-traveler; through him, his close friend,
Lee Pressman, the C.I.O.'s Stalinoid legal counsel, has been able to influence Wallace. Hannah Dorner, the national executive director of
I.C.C.A.S.P., is an even more important link. She is said to have got him
to endorse Johannes Steel, an unfortunate error which one of Wallace's
associates explained: *Henry just can't resist when Hannah calls him up.*
(See *Time,* September 9, 1946, pp. 23–25, for a good account of
I.C.C.A.S.P., including Hannah's classic reply to charges of undue Communist influence: "Says who and so what? If the I.C.C.A.S.P. program is
like the Communist line, that is purely coincidental.")

learning them at last. This puts Wallace in a most difficult position. Also the new *New Republic,* which aspires to be read by the general public but may even cease to be read by the liberal minority.

"IT WOULD BE UNFORTUNATE. . . ."

The most revealing statement—and I have already quoted it—that Wallace made on his European tour was his remark in Oslo: "It would be unfortunate for world peace if anything happens inside Russia to upset its system of government at the present time." [82] This is revealing as an endorsement of Stalin's totalitarian regime against whatever feeble opposition it may have at home. And also as an indication of Wallace's essentially conservative mentality. He cannot conceive of any radical break with existing power-institutions anywhere: for all his criticisms of present United States policies, he has never made any objection to the "American way of life"; on the contrary, like the Communists, he is loud in his admiration for American institutions and constantly presents himself as a 150 per cent American. His most concrete proposal for resolution of the American-Russian conflict was his suggestion, last spring, that Truman and Marshall meet Stalin and Molotov personally "for the avowed and announced purpose of drawing up an agreement which will cover all points at issue between the United States and the Soviet Union." [83]

Since he sees no basic defects in the present social structures of either Russia or America—or at least no defects which would prevent the emergence of a new era of world peace from a personal conference of the present heads of those states—Wallace attempts to find a way to peace without any deep social change in either nation. But, since the conflict is irreconcilable so long as both nations remain exploitative class societies, this attempt constantly results in his taking sides in the struggle despite his doubtless sincere efforts not to do so. And the side he has gradually become committed to is not that of his own country.

It is not true that Henry Wallace is an agent of Moscow. But it is true that he behaves like one.

Appendix. "Common Man" Politics
Bryan v. Wallace

HENRY AGARD WALLACE is often compared to an earlier word-intoxicated demagogue from the prairies: William Jennings Bryan. The parallels are striking. The populist crusade against "Wall Street," which Bryan led from 1896 to 1908, has found its chief modern leader in Wallace. The Great Commoner becomes the prophet of the Common Man. Both teetotalers, both religious, both addicted to Biblical imagery, both rhetoricians rather than thinkers or doers, both hated by the rich and ridiculed by the sophisticated, both even sharing the rare distinction of being accused of violating the Logan Act (Bryan was thus attacked during his 1917 peace campaign).

The comparison, however, is unfair to Bryan, who had serious convictions about the interests of the "common people" with whose cause he identified himself, and who was willing to make sacrifices for those convictions. Unlike Wallace, who has never voluntarily relinquished a post of power except to gain a higher one, Bryan resigned, on an issue of principle, the Secretaryship of State. Even that grotesque coda to his long career, the Scopes Trial, has a certain dignity about it. Bryan took his backwoods revivalism seriously: he was willing to defend a fundamentalist position on Darwinism against the formidable Clarence Darrow (who might be said to have made a monkey out of him). Wallace hedges, trying to combine revivalism with scientific enlightenment. Bryan was absurd in his attempt to prove that the Bible is literally and completely true, but one respects his moral courage—and even his intellectual consistency.

Bryan's superiority is specially marked on the issues of war and imperialism. Wallace was an uncritical propagandist for World War II, Bryan a consistent opponent of World War I; Wallace has draped imperialism—first American, now Russian—in "common man" rhetoric; Bryan struggled against the imperialism of his day. For all his religiosity, Wallace has never shown any interest in the peace movement, and his only expressed reaction to it, so far as I can discover, is the recent sneer at "namby-pamby pacificism." Bryan visited Tolstoy at Yasnaya Polonya in 1903 and was deeply impressed; he developed after this in an increasingly pacifist direction.[78] He was proud to call himself a pacifist—although, as with Wallace, there was often a startling gap between his words and his deeds. Thus, although opposed to the Spanish-American War while it was in the making, as soon as war was declared, he volunteered and led a regiment. While he was Wilson's Secretary of State, he dealt with Latin Americans on the usual armed-force basis, sending the Navy to occupy Vera Cruz and imposing on Nicaragua the treaty which later became the basis for landing the Marines. Yet in the supreme test of World War I, Bryan behaved magnificently; the Secretary of State was the most realistic and level-headed member of the cabinet. He was able to see through the pro-British propaganda which deceived Wilson and Colonel House. He saw the danger in loans to belligerents, for example, and officially declared—for the first time in history—that such loans were inconsistent with the spirit of neutrality. He tried unsuccessfully to get Wilson to protest as strongly against the British blockade as against German submarine warfare and to warn American citizens off ships carrying munitions. Finally, in the spring of 1915, Bryan reached the reluctant conclusion that Wilson's policy was pro-British and not neutral and that it was leading to war; he resigned the only high position he had ever held in his long and frustrated political career.[79] It is true that, when war was declared, Byran climbed down from this moral elevation, offering to enlist as a private and even favoring the suppression of free speech and conscientious objectors! And that, when he died, he was given a military funeral and buried in Arlington—both at his request. All this shows that, like Wallace, Bryan was an unstable and naïve personality—and also, at bottom, a good patriotic citizen, who could not understand individual resistance to the State because he believed the State was simply the voice of the people. It makes it all the more significant that the early populist demagogue should so frequently have shown up better in action than the later one.

Bryan's superiority, in a word, was due to historical rather than personal factors. At the turn of the century, populism corresponded to real mass interests and emotions; hence its prophet behaved with some consistency. Populism today is a shell which can be filled with any content, even Stalinism, and hence offers its prophet no guide to behavior. Compare Bryan's and Wallace's audiences. Bryan's favorite platform was the Chautauqua lecture: when he was Secretary of State, he was criticized for continuing to appear on the

Chautauqua circuit along with Swiss bell ringers and "Sears, the Taffy Man." The Chautauqua audience was composed of religious-minded, agrarian masses who hated "Wall Street" (Eastern monopoly capitalism) and detested the sophisticated, irreligious culture of the Eastern seaboard. But Wallace's audience is drawn from liberals who are economically well off and culturally sophisticated. For them, populism is, culturally, a phony way of making a connection with the inarticulate masses (like Josh White's songs) and, politically, a way to engage in world power-politics under attractive slogans. (Huey Long and Father Coughlin were the real populist types of our times, expressing popular interests and passions; they were denounced as fascists—with justification—by the liberal pseudo-populists.)

It is significant that, although he edited *The Commoner* for years and must have written millions of gaudy words in his time, Bryan's special skill lay in the spoken word; while Wallace, a poor orator, communicates with his audience through writing. Also that Bryan was a shrewd practical politician: his biographer, M. R. Werner, observes that he "devoted all his native cunning to the business of politics" and "reserved his native innocence for more abstract subjects." Wallace, on the other hand, who seems to lack native cunning both in practical and theoretical affairs, is a mixture of the research scientist and government administrator. In politics, he is a helpless figurehead manipulated by practical politicians. The orator and the political boss (Bryan controlled the Democratic Party for most of the 1896–1912 period) are types thrown up by the masses and skilled in dealing with them; the administrator is part of the privileged minority, just as the editorialist's appeal is only to this minority. Bryan's first big speech was an oration delivered on the spur of the moment, filling in for a speaker who didn't show up. ("Mary, I have had a strange experience," he told his wife the next morning. "Last night, I found I had power over the audience. I could move them as I chose.") Wallace's first big speech was the Free World address in 1942—actually a written editorial which he read to *his* audience of tuxedo-clad New York liberals.

Wallace is the spokesman *for,* the friend *of* "The Common Man"—separated from the masses as the lawyer is separated from his client. But Bryan was "The Great Commoner"—i.e., a common man himself.

Postscript

Throughout this book, it has been charged that Henry Wallace is fuzzy-minded to a degree unusual even in a politician; that he is constantly contradicting himself without ever admitting it; that in regard to his own public statements he is a trimmer, a hedger, and a chronic reneger; and that he lacks the guts to stand up under pressure. Much evidence has been given in support of this dim view of the Friend of the Common Man. Some readers, however, may still be skeptical. For them, especially, therefore, I reproduce below two news items that come to hand just as this book is being put on the press:

"Buffalo, N. Y., Dec. 11— . . . Early in the day, Mr. Wallace said that he would prefer Senator Robert A. Taft as President to either Mr. Truman or Governor Dewey. In expressing such a preference, the former Vice-President added quickly that he 'recognized' that Senator Taft's approach to domestic problems was that of the eighteenth century. But, he said, Senator Taft was the most likely candidate to change the nation's foreign policy, which Mr. Wallace says leads to war." (The New York Times, December 12, 1947.)

"Albany, N. Y., Dec. 12—Henry A. Wallace said tonight that he was playing a game of 'make-believe' when he told reporters he would vote for Senator Taft in preference to President Truman next year. His 'clarification' was made in a speech under the auspices of the Progressive Citizens of

America. . . . 'In my press conference yesterday, I added Taft to my list of preferences over the Truman-of-the-moment on the basis of Taft's opposition to universal military training,' Mr. Wallace explained. 'I made it clear that Taft represents the best kind of nineteenth [sic] century thinking and that the voters were entitled to a better choice than that between Taft and Truman. That point isn't very clear in the morning papers I have seen, so I am going to call a halt to the game of "make believe." . . . It is past the fun stage and I don't want anyone to seriously believe I could vote for Mr. Taft.' Mr. Wallace's original statement on Senator Taft had brought dismay and consternation to many of his labor supporters. . . . Mr. Wallace denied he had been subject to any pressure." (The New York Times, December 13, 1947.)

References

1 George Creel, "Wallace Rides Again," *Colliers,* June 17, 1944.
2 *The New York Times,* June 15, 1947.
3 *Democracy Reborn,* a collection of Wallace's speeches, edited and annotated by Russell Lord (Reynal and Hitchcock, 1944).
4 Henry Wallace, "Address to the Democratic Women's Club of Philadelphia," 1933.
5 *The New York Times,* January 13, 1947.
6 *The New York Times,* January 24, 1947.
7 *The Saturday Evening Post,* October 23, 1943.
8 *Readers Digest,* September, 1943.
9 H. N. Brailsford, "Henry Wallace," *New Statesman and Nation,* April 12, 1947.
10 Henry Luce, "The American Century," *Life,* February 17, 1941.
11 *The New York Herald-Tribune,* May 17, 1942.
12 Henry Wallace, "The Postscript," radio speech over the British Broadcasting Company network, April 13, 1947.
13 *The New York Times,* April 24, 1947.
14 *The New York Times,* June 15, 1947.
15 Henry Wallace, *Technology, Corporations and the General Welfare* (University of North Carolina Press, 1937).

16　Editorial in *The Christian Century*, April 23, 1941.

17　*Uncle Henry's Own Story of His Life* (Des Moines, Iowa: Wallace Publishing Company, 1917).

18　Russell Lord, *The Wallaces of Iowa* (Houghton, Mifflin, 1947).

19　George Peek, "In and Out," *Saturday Evening Post,* May 16, 1936.

20　Paul Ward, "Wallace, the Great Hesitator," *The Nation,* May 8, 1935.

21　Felix Belair, "Has Wallace Too Much Hay Down?" *The North American Review,* Winter, 1937-38.

22　Frank R. Kent, *Without Gloves* (1934).

23　Carl C. Taylor and others, *Disadvantaged Classes in American Agriculture* (United States Department of Agriculture, Farm Security Administration, Special Research Report No. VIII, April, 1938).

24　*Time,* December 27, 1937.

25　See Reference 18.

26　For a good account of Thomas' sharecropper campaign, see *American Messiahs* (Simon and Schuster, 1935), by "The Unofficial Observer," pp. 163-68.

27　See Reference 18.

28　H. L. Mitchell and J. R. Butler, "The Cropper Learns His Fate," *The Nation,* September 18, 1935.

29　See Reference 21.

30　*The New Deal, an Analysis* (Knopf, 1937), by the Editors of "The Economist."

31　See Reference 23.

32　Henry Wallace, *New Frontiers* (Reynal and Hitchcock, 1934).

33 Louis M. Hacker, *American Problems Today* (Crofts, 1938).

34 Robert Humphreys, "The Extraordinary Henry Wallace," *The American Mercury,* September, 1943. Henry Wallace, "What We Fight For," *Vital Speeches,* October 1, 1943.

35 Henry Wallace, *Paths To Plenty* (Reynal and Hitchcock, 1938).

36 Henry Wallace, *The Price of Freedom* (Reynal and Hitchcock, 1938).

37 Henry Wallace, *The American Choice* (Reynal and Hitchcock, 1940).

38 Rexford G. Tugwell, *The Stricken Land* (Doubleday, 1946).

39 *The New York Times,* January 24, 1944.

40 *Time,* September 9, 1940.

41 *Politics,* August, 1944.

42 Henry Wallace, "The Scientist in an Unscientific Society," *Scientific American,* June, 1934.

43 "Meet the Press" radio interview, Mutual Broadcasting System, January 10, 1947.

44 See Reference 35.

45 Speech in Seattle, Washington, July 8, 1935.

46 *The Nation,* June 7, 1947.

47 *The New York Times,* March 20, 1946.

48 See Reference 12.

49 *Time,* September 23, 1946.

50 *The New York Times,* April 13, 1947.

51 *The New York Times,* April 12, 1947.

52 *Newsweek,* April 28, 1947.

53 *The New York Times,* April 21, 1947.

54   Charles M. Wilson, "Iowa Cycle," *The Commonweal,* November 10, 1933.

55   Jack Alexander, "Henry A. Wallace, Cornfield Prophet," *Life,* September 2, 1940.

56   "The Vice-President," *Fortune,* November, 1942.

57   Henry Wallace, "Spiritual Forces and the State," *Forum,* June, 1934.

58   See Reference 55.

59   See Reference 20.

60   Beverly Smith, "FDR's Crown Prince," *American,* June, 1941.

61   See Reference 55. See also Hubert Herring, "Henry III of Iowa," *Harpers,* February, 1943.

62   Helen Hill Miller, *Yours for Tomorrow* (Farrar and Rinehart, 1943).

63   See Reference 56.

64   *Saturday Review of Literature,* March 23, 1935.

65   *Scribners,* December, 1943.

66   Speech at New York Newspaper Guild Ball, as quoted in *The New York Times,* January 7, 1947.

67   *The New Republic,* January 2, 1935.

68   See Reference 20.

69   See Reference 56.

70   *The New York Times Magazine,* January 26, 1941.

71   See Reference 56.

72   "Talk of the Town" department, *The New Yorker,* January 4, 1947.

73   See Reference 3.

74   *Time,* December 4, 1944.

75   David T. Bazelon, "The Faith of Henry Wallace," *Commentary,* April, 1947.

76 See Reference 19.

77 See Reference 18.

78 On Bryan's pacifism, see especially Merle Curti's excellent monograph, *Bryan and World Peace* (Smith College Studies in History, Vol. 16, Nos. 3–4, April-July, 1931).

79 On Bryan in World War I, see Paxton Hibben's *The Peerless Leader* and C. Hartley Grattan's *Why We Fought.*

80 *The Progressive,* June 16, 1947.

81 *The New Republic,* October 20, 1947.

82 *The New York Times,* April 21, 1947.

83 *The New York Times,* June 17, 1947.